ETHICS

ETHICS

BY

WOLFHART PANNENBERG

TRANSLATED BY
KEITH CRIM

THE WESTMINSTER PRESS
PHILADELPHIA

SEARCH PRESS
LONDON

Translated from Part I of the German
Ethik und Ekklesiologie
© Vandenhoeck & Ruprecht, Göttingen, 1977

This translation Copyright © 1981 The Westminster Press

BOOK DESIGN BY DOROTHY ALDEN SMITH

Published by
The Westminster Press®
Philadelphia, Pennsylvania
and
Search Press Ltd
Tunbridge Wells, Kent

PRINTED IN THE UNITED STATES OF AMERICA
9 8 7 6 5 4 3 2 1

Library of Congress Cataloging in Publication Data

Pannenberg, Wolfhart, 1928–
  Ethics.

  Translation of: Beiträge zur Ethik, pt. 1 of
Ethik und Ekklesiologie.
  Includes bibliographical references.
  CONTENTS: Society and the Christian faith—
On the theology of law—Theology and the crisis
in ethics—An answer to Gerhard Ebeling—[etc.]
  1. Christian ethics—Addresses, essays, lectures.
I. Title.
BJ1253.P313   241   81-13051

ISBN (U.S.A.) 0-664-24392-4   AACR2
ISBN (U.K.) O 85532 515 1

CONTENTS

1   Society and the Christian Faith   7

2   On the Theology of Law   23

3   Theology and the Crisis in Ethics   57

4   An Answer to Gerhard Ebeling   71

5   The Basis of Ethics
    in the Thought of Ernst Troeltsch   87

6   Luther's Doctrine of the Two Kingdoms   112

7   The Nation and Humanity   132

8   The Peace of God and World Peace   151

9   The Future and the Unity of Mankind   175

NOTES   199

Publisher's Note

The contributions to the study of ethics presented here in original translations were previously published by Vandenhoeck & Ruprecht of Göttingen in 1977 as the first part of the author's *Ethik und Ekklesiologie*.

1

SOCIETY
AND THE CHRISTIAN FAITH

According to the Gospel of John, Jesus answered Pilate's question, "Are you the King of the Jews?" by saying, "My kingship is not of this world" (John 18:33, 36). This saying has been the starting point of a long series of attempts to define the relationship of the Christian faith to society and to state. Christ's statement gave occasion, and apparently also authorization, for regarding this relationship as one of opposition. The classic form of this concept is found in Augustine's doctrine of the two kingdoms or cities, the "city of God" and the "earthly city." Luther's doctrine of the two kingdoms is a later variant of the Augustinian concept. In opposition to the tendencies of the medieval church toward outward manifestations and the accumulation of the apparatus of worldly power, Luther stressed the inward nature of the Kingdom of God and Christ as a kingdom of faith and of the righteous heart. By contrast, in the kingdom of the world only an external righteousness can be maintained by worldly power, which forces even evil persons to preserve the peace and to obey the law. This emphasis on the inward nature of the Kingdom of God and Christ, based on the Augustinian tradition, can be reduced to the common point of view that religion and faith are only an inner concern and therefore are not to be concerned with politics. That is an oversimplification, for not only did Augustine consistently regard secular peace as a positive good, but Luther taught that worldly power was ordained by God and that it can therefore be subject to the criticism brought to bear on it by Christian proclamation—just as on the other hand it requires for its legitimation an appeal to God. But in the modern period these points of view have been neglected because of developments that will be considered later in this discussion. The idea of the inward nature of the Kingdom of God and thus of the inwardness of religion and faith exerted much stronger influence, specifically in the direction of a total separation of faith from the tasks of politics and of the social order.

Such a radical internalizing of faith is apparently justified by Christ's statement, "My kingship is not of this world." This impression is strengthened when Jesus' words in Luke 17:21 are translated as Luther and the King James Bible translate them: "The kingdom of God is within you." But that is not the meaning of this saying. It means rather that the Kingdom of God is not a matter of future calculations, but that its future is powerfully present "in the midst of you." And when in John's Gospel Christ speaks before Pilate of the difference between his kingdoms and the kingdoms "of this world," this does not mean the inwardness of the soul in contrast to the external nature of the political world. Neither does it mean that the Kingdom of Christ is not *in* this world, but rather that his Kingdom is not *of* this world. It is also the case that according to John, believers are *in* this world, but not *of* it, because they have been born anew by the power of God (John 17:11-19; cf. 3:6-7). That the Kingdom of Christ is not of this world is expressed in the fact that his disciples do not fight to protect him from his enemies; that is, it is not a kingdom based on force. Christ's kingdom, however, does not abandon "this world" to its own devices, but claims sovereignty even over the political order. Thus the Johannine Christ says to Pilate, "You would have no power over me unless it had been given you from above" (19:11).

In the background of these mysterious-sounding statements are the points of view of the Jewish apocalyptic writings concerning the relation of the kingdoms of the world to the

Kingdom of God. The Book of Daniel (ch. 7) portrays the empires of the ancient Near East as arising one after the other out of the waters of chaos, out of the nothingness that was there before the creation of the world. The Kingdom of God, by contrast, which overcomes and dispossesses them all, comes from above, on the clouds of heaven, and its symbol is a human figure in contrast to the animal symbols, the heraldic beasts, that stand for the empires of this world. This signifies that the Kingdom of God which comes from above is what brings true humanity to its realization, that is, the hope for peace and justice which the Old Testament prophets combined with the expectation that God himself would become sovereign and establish his righteous will in the world.

Such a point of view lies behind Christ's answer to Pilate. By saying to Pilate, "My kingship is not of this world," he is answering Pilate's question of whether he is the king of the Jews. The Johannine Christ lets us know by this answer that he did not regard the Jewish kingdom, for whose restoration the Zealots were then working, as the Messianic kingdom which his message proclaimed. He was not speaking of a kingdom that would be established by human power in an insurrection against the sovereignty of the Roman Empire, but of the Kingdom of God that does not come from below, from humans, but from above, from God. This kingdom that is coming from above is already at work, because Pilate would have no power over Jesus if it had not been given to him from above. The relationship of the two kingdoms is thus not an amicable division of responsibility so that the political order would be turned over to the autonomy of the politicians and faith would be restricted to merely inner concerns. No, the Kingdom of God confronts the world at every turn as its own future. In the perspective of faith there is no provision for politics to be independent of the Kingdom of God, except in the sense of the world's opposition to God's sovereignty. In Christian proclamation, God's judgment is directed against the arrogance of the world, which is manifested especially in the striving for political sovereignty. Out of this faith in God's future sovereign rule, whose king is the risen and exalted Christ, there developed in early Christianity a dynamic that changed the world and finally led to the transformation of the Roman Empire, because it undercut its religious basis. From then on until well into modern times within the realm of Christendom there was room for political power only under the condition that those who held that power acknowledged at least in principle that they had received it "from above," so that their use of power was to be measured by the standard of the will of God, as made known in the Bible and proclaimed by the church.

It is clear that the relationship of Christianity and society in the present day no longer corresponds to this picture. The question of a *contribution* of Christians to the problems of politics and society is answered today by the counterquestion of whether such a contribution is not irrelevant. In order to deal with questions like this, we must first make it clear why it is that today the holders of political power give no more than lip service to the idea that their power has been given them "from above." In present-day political thought the separation of state and religion, the private nature of religious affiliation, has taken on basic significance for the definition of the relationship between Christianity and society. The reason for this altered situation lies in the changes that have come about in the modern period in the relationship between church and state. Thus it is important to begin by making certain observations about the relationship between church and state in Christianity in general. One of the distinctive features of the Christian religion is that it developed such a pronounced dual institutional form, a contrast of church and state, and we must keep the reasons for this in mind in order to assess the importance of the transformations that have come about in this relationship in modern times.

The Kingdom of God which the prophets promised and for which the Jews hoped is political in nature. It is the Kingdom of God, the Lordship of God himself, that will bring the final resolution of the task with which all political order is concerned, but on which all human forms of government are wrecked, the task of establishing peace and righteousness among mankind. When Jesus announced that the Kingdom of God was near, and proclaimed its presence through performing his mission, it was this political hope that was at issue. This is often forgotten, but the political theology of our own day has rediscovered it and emphasized it. This political Kingdom of God, however, became present in Jesus in a remarkably unpolitical manner. It did not bring about a reform or a revolution in the relationships of society, but it raised the question of the attitude of the individual toward God's future, the coming of God's rule. For and through the individual who already commits himself fully to God's future, God's rule has become present. This is the basis for the respect accorded to the individual in the Christian religion and also for the distinctive position of the church toward the state. Both of these assume that human destiny is a political destiny that has not been realized in definitive form and that cannot be so realized through political action, through changes in the social order. That is a conviction to which Christianity held fast even in its relationship to the Constantinian and post-Constantinian political order based on the Christian faith itself. Even a political order that is built on a Christian foundation is not the Kingdom of God. It remains provisional. And for this reason the church maintains its independence even in relationship to a political order founded on Christian principles. The church, through its proclamation and by the fellowship of its worship, imparts even now to the individual the gift of participation in future salvation, the presence of the Kingdom of God, which has never attained definitive form in the political order, even though the expectation of God's sovereign rule has political content.

At this point the Christian understanding of the faith is in remarkable agreement with the verdict of Karl Marx, that man forms a concept of a religious fulfillment of his being because his human existence has no definitive, earthly, political fulfillment.

Christianity and Marxism part company in that the Christian is unable to believe in a definitive fulfillment of humanity by means of changes in the existing structures of society. The Christian faith regards such expectations as mere illusions that lead again and again to inhuman consequences, because they justify political force by a dogmatic belief and at the same time tend to compel such belief by political means. The realization of human destiny would mean the realization in society of the destiny of all individuals. This is ultimately unattainable by human political action, because human alienation from the true nature of mankind does not depend only on external relationships; it also has an internal basis in each individual through that "missing of the mark" which Christian doctrine calls sin. It is impossible by political action to attain to a definitive realization of the human destiny of all individuals to enjoy community with one another. This is a result of the fact that in every conceivable political order the social concerns of all citizens must be provided for by a limited number among them. Thus, under the present natural conditions of human existence, it is not possible to have any political order without some humans exercising authority over others, and therefore it is not possible without conflicts between individuals and society.

Thus human destiny has not been definitively attained in political terms and cannot be attained through political action. This does not alter the fact that human destiny is in fact political, that is, it can be attained only if society includes all individuals and is for all individuals. And this is possible only where the unity of individuals is based not on human authority but on the authority of God. Only when God's sovereign rule over mankind becomes present will all individuals be animated by a common spirit in such a manner that they fully respect one another and that each finds the fulfillment of his life in his relationship to all others. Thus it is only with the coming of the Kingdom of God, as The Book of Daniel expressed it, that our humanity becomes full reality. While Jesus nonetheless revealed that for the individual the Kingdom of God was already present, and thus the future destiny of man was present, this consciousness of the presence of salvation presupposes the consciousness of the provisional nature of every present political order. The institutional independence of the church from the state keeps open in Christianity this consciousness of the provisional nature of the political order, and thereby the present possibility of freedom for the individual. If human destiny, and with it human freedom, cannot be definitively realized by political action, then individual freedom can be maintained only by maintaining one's distance from the existing political order. This occurs if there is revealed to the individual in the midst of his existing provisional relationships in the world the insight that there is access to his definitive destiny as a human being. This is the theme of faith in God as well as that of the proclamation of the church, and the church bears the responsibility for seeing that this is done by maintaining its independence from the state.

The belief that the church's duty was to indicate the limits of the state by reminding it of its provisional nature led in the history of Christianity to a situation in which the church came to regard itself as the present manifestation of God's Lordship in the world. Thus the medieval Western church through its officers laid claim to the authority of God himself over the state as well as over believers, and it did so in such a manner that it lost sight of its own provisional nature in relation to God's future kingdom. Ultimately, the medieval church broke apart because of this exaggerated claim, and the long-range effects of this break, which became definitive in the doctrinal divisions of the sixteenth century, still are determinative for the present-day situation of Christianity. Without taking account of those effects it is not possible to understand either the secularization of modern culture or the neutrality of the modern state in questions of religion and the reduction of adherence to a religious position to a private matter. If the contribution of the Christian faith to the problems of today's society can be regarded as irrelevant, the roots of this situation lie in the still-continuing doctrinal divisions of the sixteenth century.

Until as late as the sixteenth and seventeenth centuries no one questioned the assumption that the unity of religion was the indispensable basis for the unity of society. Only religious faith was considered capable of providing legitimacy for the political order as well as functioning as the criterion for the use of political power and motivating the common loyalty of citizens to their community. Even today these ideas have not lost their plausibility. Still, the political opinions that are now dominant are far removed from the thesis that the unity of society must be based on the unity of religion. The century of religious wars in Europe produced the opposite conviction, that is, that denominational conflict destroys the unity of society, and that the state must therefore remain neutral in religious matters. Originally the neutrality toward religion involved only the conflicts among Christian denominations. When religion came to be regarded as a private matter, this applied primarily only to the quarreling over differing views of Christian doctrine. In a general sense, detached from the conflicts of denominational disagreements, and thus more or less vaguely, most modern states in their constitutions have considered themselves Christian. This is also still true for the constitution of the Federal Republic of Germany. But because religious positions have become a private matter, the Christian faith has in the long run become more and more impotent in political and social issues, because Christianity has still not found any other institutional form for expressing its faith except that of mutually antagonistic denominations, however much their conflicts have lessened in intensity. The denominational conflicts within Christianity provide historical legitimation for the neutrality of the state in matters of religion. As a consequence, there is today *a priori* something subjective and arbitrary about church statements concerning state and society, and attention must be paid to statements by the churches only because they represent more or less sizable groups of voters with their convictions and special interests, but not because the voice of the church in any sense represents the spiritual foundations of our political life.

Because of the principle of the religious neutrality of the state, in modern times the belief that political order is not at all possible without religion has almost disappeared. Only a generally convincing "truth" about humans and human destiny, detached from the desires of all individuals and especially from that of those individuals who exercise political power, is able to provide the basis for the loyalty of individuals to the state. To this extent the thesis of the neutrality of the state in matters of religion rests on self-deception, if not in certain cases on conscious hypocrisy. The practical significance of religious or quasi-religious convictions for present-day governments is much greater than the thesis of the neutrality of the state in matters of religion will allow. Either the agreement of Christian convictions within a society is so strong, in spite of denominational differences, that this is the only way an adequate basis can be provided for the unity of the society, a unity whose strength makes it possible to be tolerant of minorities that hold nonconformist positions, or there has appeared in the place of the Christian faith another form of religious consciousness. In recent decades it has been necessary to take into account the various forms of civil religion—in the first place, nationalism, which is often combined with a secularized belief in being a chosen people—or other forms of political ideology, especially those represented in most recent times by the various shades of socialism.

In each of these instances a basis for a consciousness of truth that can unite society is perceived as functioning other than through the institutionalized forms of the Christian church. In the various forms of civil religion we are dealing, moreover, with forms of religious or quasi-religious faith that are competing with the Christian faith. The thesis of the neutrality of the modern state in matters of religion and that of the separation of state and religion should not deceive us on this question.

Otherwise the Christian faith will be corrupted by an unreflecting participation in the currently dominant forms of civil religion. And on the other hand, state and society, with their belief in their neutrality toward religion and various world views and in an enlightened consciousness of their freedom from ideology, will be rudely surprised by massive waves of a return to ideology. The postwar experience of West Germany seems to me to be a particularly instructive example of this. The tendency toward the elimination of ideology in public life since the early postwar period has been replaced by a new wave of ideological commitment, and this should make us clearly aware of the illusory character of the thesis that the state is neutral in matters of religion and world view. This results from an understandable human need, especially among the young, who find a long-term ideological vacuum unsatisfying, especially following the decline of the public respect that the Christian churches received in the early years after the war.

The self-deception contained in the thesis of the religious neutrality of the state is especially dangerous for the community of states based on the ideals of freedom and tolerance, which arose in the realm influenced by Christianity. The ideals of the modern constitutional state, of human rights, and especially of freedom are clearly dependent on the Christian faith, as Hegel saw with particular clarity. They represent a tolerant form of the Christian faith that is critical of authority. It was born out of the experiences of the religious wars and even today has found no appropriate institutional form, but lives on in the various denominations without institutional protection. This does not at all alter the fact that these political ideas, and especially the modern consciousness of freedom, draw their strength from the continuation of the Christian tradition. Thus a political order based on freedom is neglecting the foundations of its existence if it understands its own nature in superficial terms of a separation of state and religion. The concept of freedom is then robbed of its deeper religious content, emptied of its moral authority, banalized into the justification of private arbitrariness, and then finally surrendered up to scorn as a bourgeois illusion. When this happens the time is ripe for new forms of ideological totalitarianism. The destruction of the ultimately religious foundations of political order in the moral consciousness is then followed by its political collapse, its degeneration to manifestations of impotence and abuse, which finally could lend the appearance of plausibility to the call for its overthrow.

Today, it seems to me, a sufficiently profound discussion of the theme "Christianity and society" must be directed toward this problem. What can be done from the side of the Christian faith to afford protection from the danger of erosion for a society that is bound up with this faith, ultimately based on it, and oriented to the ideas of freedom and tolerance? The task is extremely difficult, because the modern thesis of the religious neutrality of the state has relegated the Christian faith to the sphere of merely private concerns. As a result the Christian faith is not only lacking in political power—which is naturally not the case to the same degree with the churches as representatives of groups—but because the faith has become a private matter, its consciousness of its own truth is threatened; truths that are asserted without at least a claim to universal validity cannot last.

A return to the premodern forms of the relationship between the state and religion is naturally not possible, nor is it desirable. Where dogmatic compulsion and authoritarian competition for office become the basis of government, no consciousness of that freedom can develop which is the fruit of Christian saving faith. Here the separation of state and religion as it has become accepted since the end of the age of the religious wars has its permanent justification. The lesson to be learned from the historical experience of the bloody consequences of dogmatic intolerance is that never again must political life be based on religion in such a way as to lead to the terrorizing of the human conscience and hatred of those who hold differing beliefs. The tragedy of the modern history of

Christianity is that the organizations and officials who represented the church on the threshold of this epoch failed to draw on Christianity's true sources to carry out the task of overcoming from within the dogmatic and authoritarian form of Christianity. Instead of this, as a direct consequence of the dogmatic and authoritarian understanding that the church had of the faith, those divisions of the faith arose which led to the age of the religious wars, and whose consequences forced the church more and more into a secondary political position. Continued insistence on the particularity of the denominational positions and counterpositions, each of which rejects the others, can only confine the church more irretrievably to existence in a sectarian ghetto.

The other side of this is that a reversal of the private nature of religion, which has been developing since the beginning of the modern period, can be possible only if Christianity—even in its institutional, churchly form—overcomes points of opposition that divide the denominations from each other and, without losing the identity of the confession of faith in Christ, attains to a new universality or catholicity of the Christian faith. This process would have to preserve ample room for the plurality of specific traditions and formulations of the faith in a common consciousness that they are conditioned by history and that they are merely provisional. It would also have to establish on the same basis a tolerant relationship to other religious traditions. Today Christianity can present its claim to universal truth in a manner that makes sense only if it includes the element of pluralism in its own consciousness of truth and in the oneness of its institutional form, instead of presenting it through more or less homogeneous interest groups within society.

In our century the ecumenical movement has opened the way for overcoming denominational disagreements, while at the same time respecting the plurality of developments within Christianity in the understanding of the faith, in liturgical life, and in church organization. It can reach its goal only through continuing progress in efforts to achieve mutual understanding and the mutual recognition of the various denominations. Overcoming those differences which separate the denominations of Christendom would make it possible for the church really to be a sign of the unity of humanity and an instrument for achieving that unity, as the Second Vatican Council formulated the matter in the introduction to the Constitution on the Church. The denominational forms of Christianity that grew out of the divisions in the church in the sixteenth century, however, now prevent the church from fulfilling this role in a believable manner. The significance of the ecumenical movement for the relationship of state and religion can be seen when we reflect on the degree to which the neutrality of the state in matters of religion, with all the consequences it has brought with it, is the result of that strife among the denominations which the ecumenical movement seeks to overcome. In addition, the secularization of modern culture and its alienation from Christianity, at least on the surface—which though not necessarily a consequence of secularization is still bound up in it—is to be regarded as a direct consequence of the sectarian strife within Christianity and the resulting self-assertion of the state as the bearer of a secular culture. An ecumenical understanding among the denominations in terms of mutual recognition and relationships within the framework of a new catholicity of Christianity would certainly not be able simply to reverse this entire development. It is entirely possible that an ecumenical world church would still remain a cognitive minority in the context of modern society. But it could succeed in presenting the self-understanding of the Christian church as a sign of the coming Kingdom of God, and thus as a sign and instrument of the eschatological unity of humanity, in a manner that is no longer possible for the churches that developed out of the divisions in the faith in the sixteenth century. If the churches are able to reach an ecumenical understanding, it will be possible for Christianity—late but perhaps not too late—to make good on the task, the neglect of which led to the modern splintering into denominations, the religious wars, the secularization of public life, and the reduction of religion to a private matter. By including the elements of pluralism and tolerance in its understanding of itself, Christianity will become able to present its claim to truth with new credibility, without thereby exposing itself to the charge of representing an authoritarianism that restricts freedom. Only a church that is ecumenical in this sense can expect that the political order of society might orient itself to the future Lordship of God over humanity, if it wishes to escape the judgment of God.

First of all, this means that modern democracy, as it has developed from its beginnings in England and America, must be reminded of its own religious origins. Mere human authority could be replaced, because God alone is worthy of holding authority. The people can claim the ability to exercise self-rule because all Christians share in Christ's kingship, as they do in his priesthood. The contribution of the Christian faith to contemporary democratic society must first of all consist in creating an awareness of these Christian origins of modern democracy and a recognition of democratic freedom as the expression of the Christian spirit, in order to involve it with this source from which it sprang.

In so doing, the Christian faith will, secondly, make a contribution to democratic society by revealing the danger that the secular state will collapse if it forgets the conditions of its pluralistic nature. These conditions involve a basic concept of justice that is ultimately derived from religious convictions, as they developed and were transmitted in Christianity. The Christian distinction between church and state contains the actual roots of modern secularism. It is very much a question whether a secular state that lacks the basic religious convictions which of themselves provide for a sphere of secular culture can long continue to exist. Similarly, the functioning of a pluralistic society may well depend on there being in that society a sufficient degree of agreement on what are ultimately religious issues, making it possible for freedom to be preferred over other values and thereby providing a basis for the desirability of pluralism, and thus ultimately also making possible a tolerance of positions which themselves are not based on this consensus derived from religious ideas. The U.S.A. is the society that corresponds most closely to this description. It is distinguished by a high degree of agreement concerning the value of freedom based on Christian principles, and this agreement makes possible the high degree of pluralism and tolerance that exists in that society. By the same token, wherever this religious basis is not present or has decayed, the pluralism of a free society is endangered.

In the third place, the contribution of Christianity to the preservation of a free society will involve especially the protection of the basic values of freedom and equality against distortions that could reduce them to absurdities. It is important to be aware that the principles of freedom and equality in modern democracy combine ancient Stoic elements with Christian elements in a relationship of tension. For Stoic philosophy, humans are by nature equal and also free, a condition that is destroyed only by the development of society. For the Christian faith, on the other hand, humans are equal before God, that is, they become equal in Christ, and they received the freedom which is their destiny through their faith in Christ. Human freedom and equality are seen here as a God-given destiny, not simply a natural condition. On this basis the Christian faith is able to do justice both to natural inequality and to the actual lack of freedom, in order to help humans move beyond themselves to participation in their proper destiny. This comes about through brotherhood, in the Christian sense of the word. It is only through appealing to the human destiny of freedom and equality attained by faith that it has been possible in modern times for democracy to be renewed in the face of the awareness of the reality of human inequality and lack of freedom. Where, however, the Stoic element in the concept of freedom and equality occupies the foreground, actual inequality is passed over, and unequal persons are treated, with some degree of force, as if they were equal. Freedom is not conceived of as a duty derived from the proper destiny of humans—their future salvation—but as free scope for individual caprice. The contrast between historical reality and the principles of freedom and equality leads to a loss of faith in these principles. The decline of the understanding of freedom can be illustrated concretely by the problem of property in our society and by the debate over abortion. The decline of the idea of equality is illustrated by the misuse of the concept of democratization, largely because of the fact that unequals are treated as if they were equal without making any provision for training in equality. The possible concrete contributions of the Christian faith to the solution of the problems of modern society can perhaps be defined in terms of the task of making the principles of freedom and equality concrete in a sense that has been critically refined.

In such manner Christianity could articulate anew the claims of the Lordship of God over present-day social and political life, so that this claim would not be misunderstood and shoved aside as a claim to power asserted by particular interest groups (as the denominations are regarded today) for the sake of their convictions, which are subjective and therefore not universally binding.

2

ON THE THEOLOGY OF LAW[1]

I

The question of the relationship of the Christian faith to law—or, more narrowly phrased, the question of the consequences of the Christian faith for establishing and observing law—assumed in the Third Reich an urgency unprecedented in the history of the church. Law apparently no longer had any authority of its own. This brought to light a condition that had resulted from the collapse of the concept of natural law in the nineteenth century. A positivistic understanding of law was now seen to have no defense against the misuse and falsification of law at the hands of the legislative process and the state. At that time many looked to the Christian churches, which testified through their behavior that in them there were still ultimate standards. The churches themselves felt it necessary not only to maintain intact the life of the church and the bases of that life but also, because of their Christian responsibility, to take a stand for justice outside the doors of the church.

The discussions concerning a theological basis of law were vigorous in those years, but they have not produced, even down to the present day, a comprehensive solution. The attempts in Protestant theology to find a solution fall into two groups, which stand in more or less sharp contrast to each other. On the one hand the God-given ordinances of human life, ordinances of creation or of preservation, are regarded as

23

the basis of true law. On the other hand attempts have been made to base law on the revelation in Christ.

The doctrine of the ordinances of creation goes back to Luther's definition of three spheres: the spiritual, the economic, and the political—church, marriage and family, and state. Later Lutheran theology saw these three spheres as God's ordinances of creation, in which each Christian lives. In the nineteenth century this concept found its continuation in Harless, the founder of the Erlangen school of Lutheran ethics, and it is represented today by Elert, Althaus, and other Lutheran theologians. In Reformed theology it is represented by Emil Brunner, who, however, brought the concept of the ordinances of creation into close relationship with the idea of natural law.

In contrast to the theology of ordinances, the attempts to establish a basis of law in Christological terms are comparatively recent. The stimulus was provided by Karl Barth's *Rechtfertigung und Recht*, 1938 (E.T., *Church and State*, 1939). In the postwar period the Christological basis of law was carried forward especially by Ernst Wolf, and on the juristic side by Erik Wolf and Jacques Ellul.

It seems to me that both approaches have failed to attain their goal. Neither a theology of ordinances nor deduction from Christological principles is able to provide a convincing refutation of a positivistic view of law. This is related to the fact that theology has not been able to overcome the intellectual forces that unleashed modern intellectual and scientific positivism. It involves above all the consciousness of history that developed in the nineteenth century, the discovery that all human institutions are conditioned by their times. Historical thinking appears to have dissolved every absolute standard. Traditional views of metaphysics, and those of natural law as well, have been stripped of their claims to absolute truth and can continue to have validity only as expressions of human culture in a specific age. Thus historical consciousness, insofar as it relativizes all standards that transcend temporal limits, displays a strong tendency to positivism. The intellectual and scientific positivism of the end of the nineteenth century is consequently not to be judged as just a fad, as an adaptation to the ideal methodology of the natural sciences in that period. It is that, to be sure, but its success can be understood only in terms of the spread of historical consciousness and the attendant collapse of the influence of philosophy of history. Since positivism and historical consciousness are so closely related to each other in the various intellectual disciplines, the debate with positivism can move forward only if we acknowledge the problem of historical consciousness in our approach to systematic thought. Furthermore, since historicism has brought to light, through individual research projects, a wealth of data that once discovered cannot be ignored, a further statement must be made. The only way that positivism can be overcome in the intellectual disciplines is by understanding more deeply than historicism itself has done our human involvement in history and the consequent formation of the spirit of objectivity. In any case we will not have finished with intellectual positivism as long as we avoid the problems resulting from the rise of historical consciousness. If we continue to avoid them, the consciousness of the all-permeating historical relativity will again and again threaten all artificially erected dikes based on contrived positivistic or decisionistic[2] solutions. In contemporary theology, however, the historical nature of all human reality, although it is derived from a biblical understanding of God, has by no means been able to assert its all-encompassing significance. Protestant theology since Troeltsch, especially where dialectical theology has held sway, has developed largely, as is well known, through a rejection of historical thought. It has not solved the problems of historicism but has evaded them. However, so long as theology in its own realm is unable to incorporate a historical consciousness into its mode of thinking, it surely cannot develop a concept of law that can come to grips with the historically conditioned nature of the formation of laws. Thus it is precisely at this point, in the historical variability of the forms and contents of laws, that the principal difficulty of a comprehensive basis for law is to be found. More than anything else this is what stands in the way of any renewed attempt to return to natural law. It is possible to overcome legal positivism only through a theory that makes the radical dependence of legal formations on history understandable in their concrete multiplicity and thus eliminates the tendency that inevitably leads to a positivistic attitude.

This question must be posed more directly for two contrasting approaches that Protestant theology has made to the question of a theological basis for law, even though in recent years, especially through the work of the Commission on Law of the Evangelical Church of Germany, efforts have been made to overcome the conflict between those two approaches.[3]

The theology of ordinances developed, as I have already indicated, in the context of Lutheran views of the division of society into differing ranks and classes. Despite a certain relationship to the natural law tradition, it is not necessarily connected with that tradition. The concept of ordinances does of course imply an ordering of human relationships that is characteristic of the essence of humanity and is at its core unalterable. Its difference from natural law is to be found in that it does not imply a general, abstract human nature in the ordinances of marriage and family, state and church, or even ideal rational norms in the sense of the natural law of the Enlightenment, but rather deals with the actual forms of all specific societies. Consequently we might speak here of an institutional natural law in contrast to one that is normative. Emil Brunner[4] combined normative natural law with the institutional law of the ordinances of creation. In contrast, Lutheran theologians of ordinances have sharply rejected natural law—for example, Paul Althaus, and more recently Helmut Thielicke and Walter Künneth.[5] Künneth, and especially Thielicke, pointed out the formalism of natural law, its dependence on an abstract essence of humanity that ignores all historical distinctions. The principle *suum cuique* (to each his own), for example, remains ambiguous as long as it is not determined what the *suum* is, that which is to be rendered to each person. By its relationship to the givens of society and its institutions, the theology of ordinances seems superior to an abstract natural law.

But are there really ordinances which constitute equally all forms of society that have developed in history, ordinances whose historical expressions are merely variants? Is not each concrete form of society thoroughly determined by its history? And then is not any concept of ordinances of life in society—ordinances that at least in their core maintain their identity because they are determined by human nature—merely an abstraction? Althaus protected himself expressly against the possible misunderstanding of the ordinances as unintelligible, static schemata. They are a gift we receive and tasks that are set for us.[6] Their concrete expression developed in each instance out of the historical situation. This basically admits that the concept of ordinances cannot explain the specific, historically conditioned laws governing the form of life in a society and cannot even make their functioning comprehensible. On the other hand there is the danger that each concrete historical expression of the ordinances will be controlled by the powers that happen to be ruling at that time. When this takes place, positivism is not far behind. It could take the form of a required supplement to the concept of ordinances. This difficulty, which here stands in the way of a concept of ordinances, applies also to Bonhoeffer's concept of mandates and to the concept of institutions, which is popular today.[7] Even the enumeration of the individual mandates or institutions shows their relationship to the creation ordinances. Alongside marriage and state Bonhoeffer placed work, and for Althaus and Elert "people" *(Volk)* appears as a special mandate, or ordinance. In addition, as was earlier the case in Althaus' work, a certain hesitancy has recently been noted in reference to the inclusion of church in the realm of ordinances or institutions that should be provided for persons, even apart from the historical revelation in Christ. As a designation of the entire realm, Bonhoeffer chose the term "mandate" instead of "ordinance" in order to avoid the misunderstanding that this was a given, unalterable structure and, as Althaus maintained, to make clearer the claim made on human responsibility through marriage, economics, state, and church—that is, their nature as tasks that are assigned. In addition, the concept of mandates is open to the misunderstanding that they are merely something that ought to be, and not ways of living that already have their own reality. This concept, which Bonhoeffer rejected, has been avoided by Dombois through the use of the term "institution." This term is intended to give expression to the dynamic character of the forms of law, the unity of gift and duty in their legal status. But in Dombois as in Bonhoeffer there is no real clarity as to how we arrive at a limited number of ordinances, mandates, or institutions. Are they to be found unambiguously through empirical means in this limited number of distinctive items, or are they established in some other way? Bonhoeffer did not attempt to find a derivation of the mandates, but Dombois is inclined to understand the institutions as the expression of basic interpersonal human relationships. By so doing Dombois comes again very close to the concept of natural law. Insofar as he regards the institutions as the expression of the typical social forms of relationships, we are brought back to a natural law—based not on an abstract, individualistic concept of humanity, but on a concept of humans as social beings.

Whether we are speaking of mandates, institutions, or ordinances, the main difficulty remains that of how to abstract from the social process specific basic structures that can remain unaffected by all historical activity. Is it not rather the case that what is constant and basic is merely the biologically conditioned nature of human existence, which constitutes the material of all social organization, but can be transformed by that organization in ways that have no fixed limits? In that case, our search for what is basic to all historical activity would not even need to consider the realm of social forms. It is clear that human existence fundamentally transcends its basis in nature by the creative structuring of a culture, but it is just as clear that the specific expressions of human destiny in the concrete experiences of daily life cannot—at least not yet—be identified as given and constant amid historical change. Therefore we must pose for the theology of ordinances and its modern modifications the further question: How are we to evaluate the relationship of unchanging basic structures of human life in society to their changing expressions in history? It is easy to get the impression that such constant, basic structures are assumed as obvious, so that it is possible to encounter what is truly essential. This, however, would *a priori* assign a subordinate rank to the changing historical expressions that constitute the realm of positive law. Jürgen Moltmann has recently shown what an extensive role an ideological preference for the "natural" can play over against the forms of life created by men.[8]

The unhistorical view that the structures of human relationships always remain the same, at least at their core, because they are givens of human nature, are something created, provokes a highly important theological objection to the concept of ordinances of creation. It is impossible to understand the radical nature of sin if we believe that we can empirically identify undistorted basic forms of human nature as they were created. If humans are totally sinful, then our nature as it was created cannot be found intact in some remnant, but has become fully involved in the distortion of life through sin. The defenders of the theology of ordinances have therefore generally abandoned the concept of ordinances of creation. Instead they speak of ordinances of preservation, which were given by God in view of sin in order to protect a fallen humanity from the destructive effects of sin. Bonhoeffer coined the term in 1932. It was adopted with some hesitation by Elert, and then decisively, together with the rejection of the designation "ordinances of creation" by Künneth. It was also adopted by Schlink, and the meaning it was intended to convey was accepted by Thielicke. Thielicke speaks of the "ordinances of divine patience," Schlink of the work and "command of God the preserver." There is widespread agreement that these ordinances of preservation can be recognized only in terms of Jesus Christ, because they were established for the purpose of redemption. Emil Brunner said this of the ordinances of creation, while Althaus assumed that they were naturally recognizable. If knowledge of the ordinances can be based only on Scripture, and ultimately on the revelation in Christ, we are clearly very close to a Christological basis of law. As long as appeal is made to empirically enduring structural forms of human life in community, there remains a vague remnant of the concept of a natural order of society that is given with the essence of humanity. It is vague because the term "creation ordinance," and thus the connection with the creaturely nature of man, is impugned.

Thus theological distrust of the concept of ordinances is thoroughly justified. The question of unchanging ordinances and structures is, in terms of its goal, at home in the world of Greek thought. It corresponds to a large degree with the understanding of reality held by other ancient religions, insofar as that which exists in time had meaning only as a copy of eternal prototypes. Israelite, biblical thought, however, was not oriented to a concept of an unchanging cosmos, as was Greek thought, nor did it rely on mythological prototypes. Rather, it was permeated by the reality of a God who always brings forth something new, even unheard of. Acknowledgment of God's freedom enabled Israel to hold to contingency in the course of the world and to discover the activity of God in unexpected, chance occurrences instead of taking refuge in a belief in eternal ordinances as the neighboring peoples did in their effort to escape the unintelligibility of chance events, which they experienced as meaningless and chaotic. Thus Israel understood reality, not as the reflection of prototypical relationships, of which the myths spoke, but as history. In history there was not merely the repetition of primordial archetypes but always something new that moved toward an inevitable and unexpected fulfillment. This dominance of contingency and history did not of course eliminate all continuity from the Israelite consciousness of reality. Otherwise not only law but history itself would be impossible. Still, what was permanent and enduring in events had for Israelite thought an origin in that which was contingent. It is based on a faithfulness that must continually be reaffirmed. Only faithfulness is the basis for permanence and reliability. Thus the Hebrew language used the same word for faithfulness and truth. Not only is righteousness based on the faithfulness of the community, it is defined in terms of that faithfulness. Permanence based on freely affirmed faithfulness is, however, something quite different from the concept of unalterable structures. More specifically, the concept of unalterable structures comprises only the surface of the phenomenon of permanence. It is an abstraction of the deeper dimensions, of the roots of permanence itself in contingent events—a connection that appears in the essence of faithfulness. The abstract concept of unchanging ordinances necessarily falls into the unavoidable contrast to chance events in history, which is so characteristic of the dualism of Greek thought. Faithfulness, on the other hand, is a contingent occurrence in history. It thus abolishes the contrast between the specific act and that which is constant.

At first glance the historical uniqueness of biblical thought, derived from the biblical understanding of God, is affirmed more strongly by Karl Barth than in the theology of ordinances.[9] Barth speaks of the "reliability and continuity of God's demands" (*KD* III/4, p. 18), which as such has the character of history just as much as does human activity (ibid., pp. 16ff.). Barth saw the proper field of ethics in this horizontal context, in which the vertical element of the ethical event, the "encounter of the concrete God with the concrete man" takes place (p. 28). In spite of this, Barth developed his ethics out of the vertical dimension of the Christ event, in which he understands man "as the being that is visible to us in the mirror of God's grace to men through Jesus Christ" (p. 48). He did this through an extensive analogy to the incarnation of God in Jesus Christ, instead of the opposite course of understanding Jesus Christ in terms of God's history with mankind, to which the Old Testament bears witness. Through this transformation to a Christological basis of ethics, the realm of history was again lost sight of. Prominence was given to analogies which sought to illuminate the humanity of mankind in terms of the humanity of Jesus Christ, instead of investigating that transformation of the traditional presuppositions about humanity which was brought about through the perception of Christ's humanity. Barth's individual analogies have not proved convincing, since, depending on one's starting point, it is possible to reach quite different conclusions from them. In addition, when the forms of the analogies play such a significant role as they do for Barth, the result is a loss of the historicity of the contents of law. I have already alluded to the fact that the belief that prototypical relationships in the divine sphere were mirrored by relations in the earthly realm was widespread in ancient religions, but biblical thought as a matter of principle goes beyond such schemes of prototype and copy. The biblical God is constantly bringing forth in the earthly reality things that are new, unheard of, not the shadow of things that were complete from the very beginning. For this reason if for no other, analogy can never become the basic thought-form of Christian theology. The process of drawing analogies to the Christ event is further burdened by the particular difficulty that Christological statements themselves have extensive symbolic structure.[10]

The shortcomings of Barth's efforts are not mere curiosities that are unimportant for Barth's methodology and can be overlooked, but they involve the essence of his approach. As elsewhere in his dogmatics, Barth is concerned in his anthropology (and in exact correspondence to it, in his special ethics and his theology of law) to base all statements exclusively on the revelation of Christ, specifically in the formalized concept of it as the unity of God with man. Wherever other factors were regarded as normative, Barth thought that "natural theology" was at work. This is why he was so sharply opposed to the theology of ordinances, even in the form of Bonhoeffer's mandates. Thus it is because of Barth's methodological approach that he cannot take into account in any methodological manner the actual data of the structures of legal procedures, or more comprehensively, the phenomena of these structures. To do so would imply "natural theology." Consequently, Barth can find access to legal reality only by means of analogies drawn from Christology. This often obscures the presuppositions of the concepts of law derived from the facts of history and from the logic of the data.

These remarks are not in opposition to Barth's tendency to find a new understanding of the realm of law in terms of Jesus Christ, as well as of other realms of existence. His attempt must be regarded as pointing the way to a solution. But to say that in terms of Jesus Christ we can attain a new understanding of reality does not mean that apart from him no understanding of reality is possible at all—for example, an understanding of law. Rather it means that our previous understanding of reality is transformed, and such a transformation not only involves the theoretical understanding of what is already present, but it can also become the impulse to change it. In order to focus on this transformation as such, the existing phenomena must be included in the approach to the theological question. Only so can the processes of the formation of law become accessible in their historical concreteness.

Our critique of Barth therefore does not imply a return to the theology of ordinances. In opposition to that theology the Christological basis of law is in the right insofar as theology can never uncritically adopt transtemporal, general conceptions of the nature of things. The question concerning the nature of that which exists is a Greek question, but it is not only Greek; at its core something common to humanity finds expression, and it is consequently valid beyond the limits of Greek culture. The question concerning the essence of what exists, the natural order of the phenomenal world, presupposes the idea of a cosmos that is basically unalterable, and this includes, tacitly, the Olympian gods as well. As already stated, there is no room here for an evaluation of the contingent nature of events. In terms of the omnipotent freedom of the biblical God, on the other hand, the world is seen in its totality as history, and all the nature of the creatures is seen in contingent movement. For them this is not something external, accidental, but it is fundamental to their essence and places them in the light of the eschatological future. For this reason, if Christian theology adopts the question (which is perhaps relevant theologically) of the nature of phenomena, it must subject it to a thorough, critical transformation, that is, a radical transformation into historical terms. The biblical experience of God opens the way for us to perceive the historical nature of all that exists.

History, to the comprehensive scope of which the nature of phenomena is related and thus made accessible, has its unity only in the form of God's history, the history of revelation. History cannot be secularized without distorting it and causing it to lose its unity.[11] The establishment of a Christological basis for law is thus on the right track, since the phenomena of existence can be appropriately understood, not in some type of fixed ordinances, but only in the context of the history of revelation. This does not simply rule out the Greek question as to the nature of what exists, but it reformulates it by casting it in historical terms. The source material of theological anthropology is not different from that of philosophical anthropology, that is, the phenomena which characterize human existence. Theology does not draw on some supernatural supply of materials, but it does place the phenomena of existence in a different and broader framework than does any philosophy which asks its questions in the Greek manner. In so doing, theology must undertake to become the "true philosopher," and to develop an understanding of the reality that is accessible to all in more comprehensive terms than it is possible for philosophy to attain on the basis of its Greek origins. A posing of questions in terms of a philosophy oriented to Greek thought cannot attain a comprehensive picture of the contingent nature of events.

We must not overlook the possibility that a philosophical basis for law can be established in a manner that is free from the influence of the Greek origin of philosophy. Either such an attempt will follow the historical thought of the Bible or it will proceed along the lines of the modern assertion of the independent subjective view of humanity, which had its origins in the biblical view of history. Positivism and its near relative, decisionism, must be regarded as falling into this latter category. Greek approaches continue to influence the tradition of natural law, and also those lines of thought where an essential ethical ordinance or a firm anthropological structure serves as the standard for the formation of law. From that point of view, however, significance can hardly be ascribed to the contingent nature of historical structures in actual laws. Even the concept of freedom of choice cannot bring this about.[12] In the light of the contingent nature of existing historical facts, that concept runs aground on the uncertainty of the choices in decisions that are yet to be made. Human freedom of choice, or as we can say today in more precise anthropological terms, man's constitutional openness to the world, which distinguishes humans from animals that are confined to a specific environment, limits human openness for historical actions. But in itself it still does not provide a living basis for the structures that are produced in history, since these never have their origin only in human actions. Therefore humanity's constitutional openness to move beyond every situation must itself be understood in the framework of a total reality that is historical in nature. It is no accident that mankind's specific openness to the world was first recognized in the areas influenced by the Christian faith and its understanding of the world in terms of history.

So it is only in the framework of a biblical understanding of the world as God's history that it is possible to overcome the problems of the universal variability of history, the problems of

historicism. It is certainly not the case, as Weischedel has often
asserted, that a theological basis would be binding "only on
those who share the same faith."[13] By this argument philosophy
could make easy work of disposing of theological questions. If
theological propositions were binding only on those who have
the same faith, they would be valid only as conventions. But
even moral truths claim validity, independently of whether or
not they are accepted by those to whom they apply. Theology
should claim for the truth of God at least the dignity that is
accorded to moral truths. Its statements are, if they are
theologically true, independent of whether they are acknowledged or not. They are not valid merely for a society of
believers. On the other hand, if theology is to be able to assert
such a comprehensive claim to truth, it must establish criteria
for its propositions by means of which they can be tested and
distinguished from mere assertions. Such a criterion for the
questions we are examining must be that theological statements
deal more adequately with anthropological phenomena than do
other explanations. Thus in respect to our problem, theology
must develop theories which deal more adequately with the
historical nature of law than is otherwise possible in the
philosophy of law. In view of the biblical origin of our historical
consciousness, it is safe to assume that theology can accomplish
this task. But theology must still undertake the task, instead of
orienting itself to the concept of ordinances and ignoring the
experience of history.

Several adherents of the Christological foundation of law
have made efforts in the right direction. Above all, in contrast to
the methodological demands of an exclusive Christological
effort such as that which Barth advocated, there is widespread
rejection of the attempt to derive the phenomena of law from
Christology. As early as 1946 Jacques Ellul found the
theological basis of law in principle in the covenant established
in Christ, but retained in addition elements of a theology of
ordinances (institutions) and of natural law (human rights).[14]
The eclectic nature of this procedure was by no means overcome

by his concern to find a biblical basis for his individual statements. It would have been better to demonstrate the validity of the theology of ordinances and natural law within the structure of the covenant itself. This is certainly not possible if we proceed only on the basis of the covenant, as Ellul did, and it can succeed only by taking into account the full riches of the history of God's activity, summed up in especially pregnant manner in the concept of covenant. Only in this framework does it then make sense to formulate basic legislation in terms of Jesus Christ, as Erik Wolf attempted to do in 1958 in his "rights of the neighbor." Because Wolf did not take into account the historical connections between Jesus and the Old Testament history of God's activity, he argued in an abstract manner in terms of the concept of the unity of God and man in Christ, that is, in terms of the dogmas of the early church. As a consequence, the analysis of the relation of God and man in Christ remains quite formal. There are two "original rights," that of personality and that of solidarity. On the one hand, God lays claim to the person with whom he is in relationship, and that constitutes the latter's personality. On the other hand, God, by becoming human, became our brother and our example. That is the basis of solidarity. It must be said that it is not necessary to turn to Christology for a derivation of personality in this sense. God lays claim to man in his humanity not only in the Christian faith, but wherever man is understood as being in relationship to God. The question can only be whether man as man is bound in this way to the God of the Bible, that is, whether the God of Israel is really the God of all mankind. But Wolf cannot answer this question by means of his Christological observations.

The other original right, solidarity, is in its core really specifically Christian insofar as it involves the love of God revealed in the coming of Jesus into the world and in his destiny. Still we must ask whether the idea of love has not been made so general through the concept of solidarity as to obscure its specifically Christian nature, as distinguished from the pathos of Stoic indifference. Above all, however, love here is only the norm of behavior and is not seen in its contingent activity as creative power. In spite of these criticisms, it must be admitted that Wolf has gone beyond Barth, not simply by deriving concrete legal phenomena from these original rights, but by giving them force as regulating principles derived from other sources, for the examination and formulation of legal reality. It seems to me that this provides a fruitful development for the Christological approach to a basis for law, a development in the direction of an investigation of the significance of the message of Christ for past and future concrete historical formulations of law. Thus in reality the message of Christ as the core of the Christian tradition could be a source of critical impulses for the formulation of legal reality. At least Ernst Wolf is moving in this direction when he affirms that in reference to the problem of the state, it is not at all a question of the essence and founding of the state, but of "instruction for the behavior of the Christian in the realm of actual governmental reality."[15] This formulation expresses a critical relationship to a reality that has other origins. The corrective to Barth's Christological method that is implicit in this forces us, however, to raise anew the whole question of the reality of law in the framework of an examination which from the outset involves the established data of general anthropology.

II

In the light of all that has been said, a theology of law cannot begin with various principles, not even specifically theological principles, if it wishes to establish the basic principles of law. Rather, the opposite approach must be taken, presupposing a general anthropology of law, but only as a provisional aspect which must be replaced by an understanding of humanity gained in the concrete course of human history. A theology of law is on its own ground only where the formulations of law are seen in historical perspective. But it cannot begin there. A historical approach always presupposes other, comparatively abstract and provisional, aspects of mankind and human behavior in respect to man's basis in nature and to man's social relationships. But we must go beyond these aspects of a biological and a formally sociological anthropology and attain an understanding of man that encompasses human nature in concrete events in the life of the individual. It is the retelling of human history which brings us as close as it is possible to come to that which man is in concrete reality.

Therefore we must begin with a comparatively abstract question, derived from the course of history, concerning law as a phenomenon of human life in society. As a beginning, it can of course not give us the final picture of things. Law here is an unavoidable feature of human community. It is not true, as has so often been asserted since Tönnies, that a naturally developed community (*Gemeinschaft*) and a society structured by law (*Gesellschaft*) stand in opposition to each other. Every community, if it is to endure, requires a firm structure, an ordering of life by definite mutual duties of its members toward one another.[16] This holds true for a small group just as much as for comprehensive and complicated societies. Thus the legal forms of life in community develop and its nature changes as the roles and status of the individual members are differentiated to form a network of relationships and become established in reciprocal recognition. This is the way in which relationships of leader and follower are formed. Such forms of life, which are constituted by mutual recognition, are already in themselves legal relationships, even when they are not expressly formulated as such.

As the form that has always characterized human community, law is concerned with the question of the nature of our humanity, the fulfillment of which is sought in human life together, whether it is in the framework of an existing society or, in dissatisfaction with that society, in a revolutionary drive toward a new formulation of life in community. In the search for our human nature, law—as the form which human society takes on—is involved with the idea of God. I will demonstrate this by starting from the concept of human nature, then formulating on that basis the idea of God, and only after this detour returning to the question of law.

What mankind is, is never finally determined in the sense of a fixed concept of the human essence; in contrast to all animals, humans are essentially "open." Man has the task of "constituting himself."[17] Unlike the animals, man is not confined through instincts to a limited environment. Rather, his "openness to the world" means, as behavioral anthropology[18] has shown, that man must always orient his drives. He seeks to accomplish this through gaining experience of his world. Man primarily seeks to determine what he wants and what he really is by means of the world in which he finds himself. To be sure, the world as he finds it is not able to satisfy his nature (as the sum of his drives). So he transforms what he finds around him. He proceeds to construct an artificial "environment," or better, a cultural world.

Man has therefore been called a cultural being. This is correct in that existence is for man essentially a task to which he must constantly seek to give form. But on the other hand, no cultural formation can have for man the significance that the given natural environment has for animals. Human questions go not only beyond nature but also out beyond all cultural accomplishments into that which is still open. Formation of culture can therefore not be the ultimate goal of human nature, but it can be understood in its own variability only when we recognize that to which the human question is directed, beyond man's natural environment and even beyond the cultural forms existing at the time.

This consideration leads to the conclusion that we cannot replace natural law by a cultural law, under which the judge in his decisions would ultimately be bound by the highest principles of the culture of that time. To be so bound would threaten the openness of human existence. Our entire cultural heritage constantly confronts the question of whether or not it can be preserved. Therefore the function of the judge as a creator of law is to be emphasized. Culture itself, which includes not least of all the form of community life, finds itself in ceaseless transformation, and to this, as concerns the formation of law, the judge also makes his contribution.

The so-called openness of man to the world is not openness for any already existing world, but an openness that goes beyond any framework of the world that may take shape. Further, it is not primarily a matter of creative excess, but of necessity. Man seeks his nature beyond everything that he finds at hand, because he does not already have his nature and cannot find it in the world as it exists, either in nature or in culture. Openness to the world is basically a questioning. Man does not merely ask questions here and there, but in the entire course of his existence he is himself a question that has not yet received its answer. Man's openness therefore points him beyond the world to a reality which is itself not the world, but which first of all includes life in the world in the form it takes at that specific time. It points man to an unknown reality for which he is seeking, because only in relationship to it can his nature come to fullfillment. If such fulfillment were *a priori* impossible, if resignation were the only answer to the question of human nature, then this question, without which human existence cannot be fulfilled, would be silenced. So man, because of the ultimate ground of his essence, cannot avoid asking what his nature is, asking beyond the world, in the expectation that this question of his will find a reality as its answer. To this reality for which man in the questionableness that permeates his existence is seeking, language gives the name God.

The structure of this approach which we have been following is characteristic for the manner in which thought in its many different forms has spoken about God. In the modern period, thought about God begins not with the world, but with man, and God is the presupposition of man's existence. Nicolas of Cusa, Descartes, and Kant and his followers always thought of man as being able to conceive of himself in his freedom only by presupposing the existence of God.[19] To be sure, they thought that with this insight they had already found the answer to the question of God. They believed they could say how God was to be thought of, when all they had thought of was the questionableness of human existence, and God as the unknown reality to which man in his questioning nature is open, open beyond the limits of the world.

Theologians are in the habit of quickly labeling any such considerations as "natural theology." The label does not fit here, because God is thought of in terms of man, not in terms of the world, but above all because here is described only the open questioning of human existence for the answer not yet given, without there being any answer found in our realm of history. For the direction from which the answer is to be awaited, we provisionally use the word "God." What God is remains for the time being unknown. God is at first only a name for the unknown reality for which man is seeking, whether he knows it or not, insofar as he shares in the openness which characterizes his behavior as specifically human, and insofar as in this questioning he stands in need of a fulfillment which he has not already attained, which he cannot attain on his own, but which from time to time comes to him in provisional form out of the future of the reality for which he is seeking.

This way of speaking of the character of human existence as a question and of God as that for which man-the-question is seeking, was characteristic of early dialectical theology, and it was carried further by H. J. Iwand in his lectures, published posthumously.[20] These discussions always correctly emphasize that man cannot give the answer to the question which he himself constitutes. Who God is cannot be derived from the openness of human existence. This affirmation distinguishes our position from that of modern subjective metaphysics, which has paralleled our discussion thus far. But as has been said, the force of its ideas points (in a manner different from what it itself intended) only to the questionableness of human existence, especially since this question is not self-contained, but like all questions looks beyond itself for an answer. What this answer is, what God is, the anthropological formulation of the concept of God is unable to say. The answer to man's question can be given only through the experience of the reality which this question is seeking.

The experience of the reality of God, not only as it has been found historically in the varied forms of the religions but as it also lies at the basis of philosophical and artistic portrayals of the reality of existence, always involves the experience of reality as a whole. Man's question about his nature is always concerned with the whole of the reality in which he finds himself. From there he seeks also to understand himself, thanks to the specific objectivity of his experience of the world which allows man to linger in the world of the phenomena relatively free of his emotions, so that from the phenomena he can look back at himself in order to see himself in the context of his world. The more comprehensive the context in which man finds his place, the more reliable the resulting picture will be. Man's question about his nature thus involves the question of the whole of reality.

The totality of that which man encounters in his environment does not have its unity in itself. It does not constitute a whole in itself: Only in the light of that which man does not encounter, but for which he seeks because of his nature, does that which he does encounter find its unity. Thus on the one hand there is the unencounterable, unknown God (although the question that man himself constitutes points to that God), and on the other hand the world as that which we encounter as closed and complete in the light of that question. The two are experienced together. A specific understanding of the world always corresponds to a specific understanding of the reality of God, and vice versa.

We can see the correspondence between thoughts about God and our understanding of the world most clearly in the light of the contrast between a cosmic and a historical understanding of the totality of reality. The idea of the cosmos, like that of history, involves the whole of reality, not merely some aspects of it. In thinking about the cosmos we think of the deity as the origin of the present world order. The idea of an unchanging order of the phenomena is a constitutive element in our understanding of the world. The essence of phenomena is always already present in or behind them. It is a different matter when the whole of reality is understood as history. There attention is centered on the unexpected way in which events surprise us by breaking into our world. Thus reality is understood in terms of the omnipotent God of Israel. For this mode of thought, happenings, figures, and events do not have their essence in themselves; it is only the future that will decide what they really mean. Only the final outcome of all that occurs will finally reveal the true meaning of individual figures and events in the course of history; reveal, that is, what they really involved. Despite the contingent nature of all events, Israel experienced a continuity among individual events, because the Israelite people were living in anticipation of the future that God would bring. Thus from each new experience they could look back to their past, to their heritage, and say, "This was in and of itself open to the future that God has for us." That which was so explicitly present in Israel can also be affirmed in a more general sense of the continuity of all human history. We can reaffirm our heritage from the past, because the past pointed beyond itself to the future.

Thus the question of the nature and destiny of man brings God and the whole of reality together, because humans search for their identity in the whole of reality, in that which exists in its reality only in the presence of God. All the answers to such questions given on the basis of our investigation of reality are religious answers, even when they take the form of philosophy, ideology, or works of art. But the answers of the religions are not all of equal value. Their claims can be subjected to examination in the light of the relationship of the question of God to our understanding of the world, as set forth above. Every experience of the reality of the unknown God must be substantiated by an understanding of the world, including human existence in that world. In this sense the question of the truth of the biblical concept of God also takes on meaning. It must be shown to what degree the whole of reality and thus also of human existence can find a more profound explanation in terms of the God of the Bible than it can find anywhere else. Only in this way can the assertion that the biblical God is the true God be substantiated.

It is now time to ask what all this has to do with law. Establishing the reality of the existence of the God of the Bible involves also the reality of law. If the formation of law always involves a "preliminary outline of the historical nature and destiny of man"[21] then it is clear that human openness as openness to God does have something to do with law. The search for the unity of reality, which is involved in the human question about God, concerns not only the unity of the world outside the human sphere but first of all the unity of humans among themselves. We are searching for human destiny as something common to all individuals. It is not that each one has a specific destiny that is his or hers alone; rather, the destiny of all humans as humans is one, and therefore we seek together for it and give it form, at least in provisional expressions in our life. Because all humans seek their destiny as something they have in common, it is unavoidable (and also appealing and deeply satisfying) that we should come to an understanding among ourselves. We search for the truth only because the truth about God, the world, and humanity can never be one's own private concern, but is the concern of all. Even the fact that we speak about mankind and not about this or that individual can be justified only by reference to the common destiny of us all.

Human nature and destiny are expressed in various provisional forms through the formation of concrete societies. This is why the society to which one belongs has such power over the individual, even including the individual conscience. In the last analysis it is only in terms of the unity of human nature that we can understand why humans join together to form societies. The external pressures that force persons to form such associations should not be underestimated in their significance for the development of life in community. But they only provide the stimulus that leads people to join together for common efforts and do not justify us in regarding such stimuli as the exclusive cause of the formation of communities. The fact that concrete societies are always merely provisional expressions of human destiny is primarily due to their being specific and particular forms. Smaller societies are always related to more comprehensive ones, and thus ultimately to the unity of humanity. But we have never thus far been able to arrive at a form of law that would provide for humanity as a whole a definitive form of life together. Even if we could attain the great goal of a community of law that included all mankind, there would still remain conflicts among the particular societies, such as those which in the existing political states pose, from time to time, a threat to the form of the whole. Because the destiny that is common to all humans has not thus far found definitive expression in any existing society, conscience, which on the one hand binds the individual to his society, on the other hand impels him out beyond it.

Wherever law formulates the conditions of human community in a concrete situation and measures the individual and his conduct by that formulation, then, as we have seen, this always takes place in the framework of the comprehensive question of human destiny. This question includes God, the totality of present reality, and the necessity of human community (as a form that expresses the unity of human nature in all persons).

From ancient times there has always existed a close connection between law and religion. This connection—as should be clear through the considerations dealt with above—is not something external to the nature of law which could be left behind as belonging to an outmoded mythological period. Rather, the legal ordering of human communities is ultimately binding on an individual as a person only with reference to the deity. Beyond the reach of the power of the state to enforce compliance, the only reality that obligates man with ultimate urgency to preserve society is that which comes from God. Consequently it is realistic to look for a theological basis of law. Only so can human society escape the threat posed for it by human arbitrariness. Consequently the anchoring of law in religion often has a conservative significance, but this is by no means necessarily the case. It can also provide the impulse to the formation of human relationships that would be worthy of mankind, and this must always be the case when our understanding of God includes the relation of human destiny to the future, a future that has not been exhausted by any already realized form of human life in community, but remains open, as is characteristic of the biblical idea of God.

The relationship between law and religion has two aspects: first, human destiny forces us to live together in society, because individuals can comprehend and give form to their destiny only as something common to all; and second, the common destiny of mankind in its specific openness beyond all realization in this world points to God. Thus wherever humans are caught up in the reality of God, they perceive their nature as something common to all, and each individual is impelled to express his community with his fellow humans. Only in such community, even though it is always only in a provisional form, can we live in the sight of God in accordance with our nature.

This enables us to attain a proper understanding of the meaning of Israel's religion for all humanity. It was there that the connection between human community with God on the one hand and human community under law on the other found its classical expression. Israel's religion took the form, as has no other, of the religion of the law of God. God's covenant with Israel formed the basis for the community of the Israelites with one another under law. This gave expression to the truth that the destiny of humans to be in fellowship with God cannot be achieved apart from the community of humans among themselves, just as the converse is true, that the community of humans among themselves signifies the true fulfillment of human destiny only in connection with human openness to God.

The relationship between community with God and a community of law, as it found expression in the religion of Israel, contains within it the dynamic of a historical movement. Since God's covenant with Israel formed the basis for the community of the Israelite people under law, God's faithfulness to his covenant, his justice, is to be fulfilled by his bringing to completion the whole human community under law. This involves not only the fulfillment of community under law within Israel but also its extension to all humans everywhere. Just as God's covenant is directed through the choice of Israel to all the nations, so the eschatological community of law which Israel was waiting for God to establish was to include all nations. The Kingdom of God becomes also—because it is God's kingdom—the kingdom of true humanity. Therefore the eschatological kingdom in The Book of Daniel is not identified by animal symbolism, as were the preceding kingdoms, but by a human symbol. This is the origin of the concept of the Son of Man in apocalyptic.[22]

With this concept is also associated the figure of the Messiah, the Christ. Originally "the Anointed" was a title of the Israelite king, who was responsible for the community of the people under law.[23] The king was the one "whom God had set up as guardian of law and justice, to whose care the poor and the victims of injustice were commended,"[24] even though it was not he but the priests and elders who were the normal custodians of law in the local communities. Since not only in the northern kingdom of Israel but also in Judah in the South the actual development of life under law called forth a vigorous prophetic critique (in the North, from the time of Amos, and in Judah from that of Isaiah; cf. Isa. 1:21-26 and 27-31), this development became connected in Judah with the hope for a future king who would enforce the law, because of the belief that God had chosen the dynasty of David. The prophet Isaiah's concept of the future time of salvation was essentially that of a peaceful kingdom, in which the ruler enforced the law.

And his delight shall be in the fear of the Lord.
He shall not judge by what his eyes see,
    or decide by what his ears hear;
but with righteousness he shall judge the poor,
    and decide with equity for the meek of the
        earth;
and he shall smite the earth with the rod of his
        mouth,
    and with the breath of his lips he shall slay
        the wicked.
Righteousness shall be the girdle of his waist,
    and faithfulness the girdle of his loins.
                                        (Isa. 11:3-5)

It is here in Isaiah that the origin of the Jewish Messianic hope is to be found, and we see how closely this hope is connected to the perfected community under law, not only in respect to Israel, but also by including the nations. Because the Messiah establishes justice in Israel, the other nations will seek out the throne of David (Isa. 11:10) and "out of Zion shall go forth the law" (Isa. 2:3).

In the postexilic period, the leaders of the Jewish community attempted to establish the new Jerusalem on the basis of the divine law that had been handed down. Israel's legal traditions were regarded as valid and put into force without any temporal limitations, in spite of their relationship to the historic conditions under which they had arisen. Even at that time this meant an artificial observance of a long outdated positivism. The theocratic demands of this undertaking came into conflict with groups that had preserved the prophetic hopes for the future and were unwilling to see the fulfillment of those hopes in the wretched existence of the postexilic community. The heart of this conflict was the question of whether any particular legal community could claim that it was the final realization of divine law. In any case, this eschatologically oriented circle could see in any legal community that did not include all peoples—as the hope-filled picture of the feast in Zion at the end of time expressed it (Isa. 25:6-7)—only something temporary, and maintaining the future hope became for that circle the decisive criterion for membership in the fellowship of the righteous.[25] This expressed the truth that recognition of the provisional nature of all established legal systems is one of the conditions of its own integrity. Thus the eschatological expectation of a better community of law in the future constitutes the condition for justice in the future. In this future expectation, law is interrelated in a special way with its divine foundation, because only the future realization of justice under law will correspond completely to the will of God. The prospect of such thinking can be found in Ernst Bloch's recent book, *Naturrecht und menschliche Würde* (1961), which interprets the concepts of natural law as anticipations of a better future.[26] It must be noted that this aspect has not traditionally been in the foreground of the thought of proponents of natural law, but that they were rather seeking to formulate law that was true for all times and places, even though it was not universally in force, but instead was frequently distorted. By contrast, the relationship to the future is explicitly constitutive for the Israelite expectation of the Kingdom of God. Ernst Bloch, by interpreting the teachings of natural law from this perspective, is justified in the sense that this makes visible the actual meaning, the truth of natural law, of which the originators of the doctrines of natural law remained largely unaware. In terms of the eschatological hope for justice the truth of the teachings of natural law is revealed in greater depth than was possible in terms of its own understanding of itself.

The Jewish sects of the postexilic period still had not realized the full significance, for the applicability of traditional law, of the fact that the hope for the future manifestation of God's lordship and the adapting of one's own conduct to that hope were the conditions of true righteousness in the present. The hope for the coming Kingdom of God constituted for the pious Jew only the framework—though an indispensable one—within which he lived according to the prescriptions of a law that had been transmitted in a multiplicity of fixed regulations. Living according to the law that had grown up during the centuries before the exile remained for him the condition of his own future participation in the Kingdom of God. The conflict over the eschatological hope only led to the separation of certain groups of the pious, such as the Qumran community, from the rest of the nation in order to establish in the wilderness a separated theocratic community that was oriented to the law in the same way. But such sectarian splintering did not represent the true consequence of the realization that in the present the eschatological expectation of God's kingdom already constituted the condition for justice. The meaning of this realization is that belief in the coming of the Kingdom of God is the only condition for participating in it, so that the keeping of the traditional law in addition to that belief is not essential for righteousness. This conclusion was first made clear in the message of Jesus. The expectation of the coming Kingdom of God, the turning to God, was now to be the only condition for righteousness. This is why Jesus left the wilderness to return to civilization. Because trusting in the coming Kingdom of God was sufficient to make people righteous in the sight of God, Jesus could announce forgiveness of sins to those who believed his message that the Kingdom was at hand. They did not need to leave the realm of their everyday life, but only to incorporate into that life a trust in God's future. Thus Jesus became proclaimer of God's fatherly love, which brings the gift of salvation even to the "publicans and sinners."

God's love for sinners is the bridge over which Jesus' eschatological message leads to a new establishing of law among humans. In their trust in God's future, humans can preserve for themselves the fellowship with God they have received as a gift, but only if they forgive others as they themselves have been forgiven. Through the message of Jesus, God gives to humans the assurance of fellowship with him, the fulfillment of their destiny, their salvation. But it is basic that he gives it to everyone, if one is willing to accept it. Therefore the love of God impels all those who receive it to overcome all that separates them from fellowship with their fellow human beings.

A further question. What is the significance for all mankind of Jesus' violating the bounds of late-Israelite piety in respect to the question of law, that is, the question with which the Jewish religion found itself so passionately concerned? The first point to be mentioned here is liberation from the tradition of fixed statutes which had long since lost their specific relationship to justice or were not unconditionally binding. To be sure, from the future of God we receive the command to regulate human life in community according to law, but the form that was at one time appropriate for this life cannot be permanently binding; for each situation it must be determined anew in terms of God's future. Otherwise, traditional law will become mere external regulation that not only tyrannizes the people but also fails to lay claim to them in the depths of their being. Jesus raised both these objections to Jewish legalism.

The second point is that we become able to recognize how it is that, in terms of God's future, mankind can practice justice. Just as God gives himself in fellowship to those who trust in his future, that is, in love, so they in turn must preserve their fellowship with God by opening up the future to their fellow men and women by showing the same love that God has shown to them, and not to them alone, but to all. Thus the power of the love that streams out from God's future brings about the community of all mankind. Through God's love his future lordship is already present in the work and the message of Jesus. Thus Jesus is the Messiah whom Israel was expecting, who will establish a complete community of justice among mankind, and it is right and proper, in keeping with the eschatological meaning of the coming of Jesus, that after Easter his followers carried his message to all nations. The church that arose in this manner must understand itself only in the context of the Israelite expectation of the Lordship of God. This is not to be done in the sense of a theocracy, as if in the church the complete community of justice under law had already taken on its final form, but in the sense that it has received from God's future one new impulse after another for the structuring of human life in community. The church is not yet itself the perfect society, just as the Kingdom of God has not come in its final and perfect form. But it is the community of those who await the coming of the Kingdom and are now living in a manner appropriate to that expectation. In this sense, the church is living on behalf of all mankind, because according to the will of God, according to the expectation of Israel, all the nations are to become a part of the eschatological society under law. Thus the fellowship of the church which confesses Jesus Christ will, if its confession is genuine, seek to make the power of the love that establishes justice effective in the formation of every human society.

This is therefore ontologically of extremely great significance for law, because the love which Jesus Christ revealed demonstrates that it is the power which underlies all formulations of law. That is, through this love people recognize that which confronts them, incorporate it into their own lives, and establish thereby a community which did not previously exist. Hans Dombois recently termed the concept of "acknowledgment" the basic category of law (along with the "responsibility" which corresponds to it and is to be perceived through "acknowledgment").[27] In reality, every form of human community, which invariably has the nature of a free creation, depends on the mutual recognition of its members. In sociology, this meaning of recognition has been worked out with especial clarity by A. Vierkandt. The roots of these and similar lines of thought in modern philosophy of law are to be sought, if I am not mistaken, in Hegel. In his *Phenomenology*, Hegel stated: "Self-consciousness arises only through being recognized."[28] And at the beginning of the chapter on law in the *Encyclopedia* it says that I have "the existence of my personality" only in relationship to other persons and in the state of "being acknowledged" by them.[29] The origin of these thoughts in Hegel's works is found in the early discussion of the "spirit of

Christianity and its fate," where Hegel discovered in the Christian idea of love the overcoming of the separations that had resulted from modern developments. Love brings about the mutual acknowledgment of those who have been separated, and thus produces unity in the midst of diversity.[30] Thus for Hegel the universally valid phenomenon of acknowledgment, which lies at the base of all formulations of law, has its roots in Christian love.

By constantly creating new forms of human community and uniting those who have been separated, love produces positive law. The law that is produced by love is not some ideal order with a claim to timeless validity (and thus, in this sense, it is not natural law) but the specific, concrete solution of concrete problems until something new arises; that is, until a new situation demands new solutions. A theological foundation of law has thus been oriented to the revelation of God's love in Jesus Christ and involves the possibility of positive law through the love that establishes communities, not with blueprints of an ideal order of law that once and for all would be guaranteed through revealed theology. For this reason, the basing of law in love cannot result from the commandment to love, because this has only the function of showing persons the way into the realm where love holds sway.

The action of love that is mutually acknowledging and establishes community is indispensable, because it is not self-evident that the human need for community and for the aid that community provides for living one's life will be met. Such fulfillment cannot be derived from anything else, and it has always the character of a positive, creative formulation. Love is creative. In it God's future gains power over individuals and enables them to fulfill their destiny in relation to one another. Here the creative freedom of the imagination is alive. Love discovers possibilities for promoting understanding, for the life together of those who are apparently hopelessly estranged, and possibilities for reintegrating even lawbreakers into society.

When we speak of the creative imagination of love in the

formulation of law, we are not to think of a fawning love that knows no responsibilities and creates no obligations. The ideas of our imagination must prove themselves by meeting in the best possible way the issues that confront us and overcoming them in the best possible manner. To this extent, our imagination of love is also the mainspring for truly rational behavior.

It seems to me that only in this way is the "daily transformation of law" (Maihofer) possible. The empty thought of the openness of humans is unable to lead by itself to the formation of any content for the reality of law. It all depends on what fulfillment this human openness receives from God, from the future of human destiny. Only in terms of our current understanding of God and of reality as a whole is it possible to say what humans are in the light of their destiny. In this respect the Christian understanding of God, of the world, and of man in the world has the advantage in that it does not close off our human openness to the future, but rather for the first time makes it fully possible. It is no accident that the modern anthropological view of openness to the world originated with the theologian Herder. On the basis of the Christian understanding of God, humans are seen as those who are called out of the world, but who through creative love for the world and their fellow humans return to it. On the basis of this answer which a specific history of mankind gives to the question concerning human destiny, a concrete formulation of law becomes possible, a formulation which constantly revises existing law in the light of the eschatological destiny of mankind.[31]

One final word. As love is being worked out it is always confronted by the problems of life, by the antagonisms in the structure of reality. To go back to one of Fichte's thoughts, it might be said that this reality has been created by God as the raw material of love, as that which mankind should not remain, but rather should overcome by the power that forces us out beyond that which is present into that which now has "no place," utopia, in order to prepare for it a place on this earth. Humans should not simply "let things run their natural course." If humans in pursuit of their destiny do not move beyond what is present, the failure to do so is a manifestation of sin, of egocentricity, of dependence on what we find existing in our own selves and in our world.

The antagonism in the structure of the world is a feature of its finiteness. It also was created by the God for whom humans are searching in the questionableness of their existence. The oneness of human destiny can become reality only when it does so together with the oneness of the world. But the world is not yet completed. What confronts mankind in the world is to be surpassed day by day in the direction of that future of God which has not yet appeared, but which will put a final end to these antagonisms. That is the future we hope for in the metaphor of the resurrection of the dead, the future that is the goal of the life of love.

3

THEOLOGY
AND THE CRISIS IN ETHICS[1]

I

The year 1879 saw the appearance of Wilhelm Herrmann's first great work, *Die Religion im Verhältnis zum Welterkennen und zur Sittlichkeit* ("Religion in relation to our knowledge of the world and to morality"), subtitled "A foundation for systematic theology." The book had lasting influence on the school of Ritschl. The exclusive nature of its ethical foundation for theology in continuity with Kant was much more characteristic for Herrmann than it had been for Ritschl's original thought. Ritschl, in the first edition of his major systematic work, had emphasized that the Christian idea of God can and must be shown to be scientifically necessary for our theoretical knowledge of reality, specifically in reference to the unity of our understanding of reality. Such unity cannot be attained in any other way (p. 29). Under the influence of Herrmann, however, Ritschl, in his third edition (1888), modified these ideas, so reminiscent of Lotz' theistic metaphysics, by placing more stress on the Kantian, moral concept of God and by an ethicistic narrowing of methodology.[2] Herrmann is the classical representative of this position. In his 1879 work he sought to free theology from all connections with our knowledge of the world. In the then-existing situation, this naturally also meant freeing it from any threat of positivistic attacks on the metaphysical tradition and especially from any possible collision with the discoveries of modern science. For Herrmann, the Christian faith was closely connected with the realm of morality: "If religious faith as a whole cannot be legitimized as the form of intellectual life which corresponds to the moral personality, then no dogmatic proof of it is possible" (pp. 275f.). Thus Herrmann, in contrast to the indifference that reigns in this matter today, still regarded a dogmatic proof of the truth of the Christian faith as necessary, because for him the truth of Christianity[3] was not confined to a mere "kerygmatic" assurance but was still a serious concern for "free judgment." At that time Protestant theology had not yet abandoned its claim to universal validity. Herrmann differed from his opponents Lipsius and Luthardt only in that he wanted to establish such a dogmatic proof solely on the basis of our moral consciousness and no longer on that of a theoretical consciousness. That this narrowing of scope was the beginning of the end for the truth claims of Christian theology could not then be perceived, at the high point of Neo-Kantianism, on which Herrmann's work was dependent.

Specifically, how did he understand morality as the basis for proving Christian truth? Not in the sense of equating morality with religion, but by taking morality as a supplement to it. In opposition to Kant and the old rationalism he did not wish to regard religion as a product of moral consciousness, but as its independently established condition, and, moreover, as a condition, not of the validity of the ethical imperative, but of the concrete living of an ethical life.[4] In contrast to Kant, he regarded the source of religious experience as historical revelation, not morality (pp. 365ff.). "This revelation of God, to which we freely commit ourselves, is the man Jesus in his lifework" (p. 390). But the view that God is revealed in the person of Jesus, and above all in his "inner life" (p. 387), must, according to Herrmann, be validated by our moral consciousness. One's personal spirit cannot bow before anything except a moral personality. "Consequently the revelation of God to which we submit can be nothing else than the moral personality in which

Jesus confronts us" (p. 400). To be sure, Jesus' moral authority, his proclamation of the true God, "can bring persons together in a community of trust in him only when it at the same time removes from them the yoke of the law, while teaching them to understand the law in all its depths and bringing them to acknowledge its validity." This is because without the message of forgiveness, the moral greatness of Jesus would prevent us from attaining to any assurance of salvation and would lead of necessity to extinguishing "the ability to develop religious belief" (p. 396). Herrmann summarized his approach as follows: "We have shown that the nature of the revelation in Christ consists in his moral majesty and its indissoluble connection with his forgiving love toward us" (p. 397). The understanding of the significance of the revelation in Jesus is, as Herrmann expressly emphasized, "dependent on the well-known vitality of moral consciousness" (p. 432).

In his later works, Herrmann expressed with even greater clarity, if that is possible, the ethical basis of theology. In his major work, *Der Verkehr des Christen mit Gott* (1886), he says that "the only God who could reveal himself to us is one who in our moral battles shows himself as the power to whom we are truly subject inwardly. This is imparted to us by the revelation of God in Jesus Christ."[5] And here we are told once more that the "precondition for a religious act" is the "moral attitude of man, the recognition that everything within him should bow before the Good" (p. 169). That is, however, only the precondition, because "the consciousness that morality itself places demands on us" must be supplemented by "the historical fact of the person of Jesus and his power, grasped in an individual experience" (p. 82; cf. p. 287).

Herrmann's ethical proof of Christianity has had far-reaching influence down to the present day. At times the influence was largely underground, but in recent years it has become clearly visible again. In contrast to Karl Barth, Rudolf Bultmann never abandoned the theological concepts of their common teacher. He did criticize Herrmann, but less for the ethical basis of his theology than for his relating theology to the historical Jesus, to the "inner life of Jesus." Bultmann, in his 1927 debate with E. Hirsch, emphasized that Jesus "as a 'thou' in the sense of a fellow human being is a thing of the past" and therefore an encounter with his "inner life" is no longer possible. And therefore, by this line of argument, Herrmann "unwillingly" ended up trying to present the "inner life of Jesus" as a datum that can be found in world history.[6] In fact, Herrmann, with his emphasis on the historical Christ,[7] was drawn increasingly into the quest for the historical Jesus.[8] Bultmann rescued Herrmann's concept from this bind by substituting the word of proclamation for the "inner life of Jesus." But nevertheless Bultmann remained quite close to Herrmann when he said, "The gospel presupposes the law that was given to me together with my historical existence" (p. 109). The fact of the law was first "disclosed" through the word of proclamation itself (p. 109), insofar as the proclamation "uncovers" the reality of our life under the law (p. 110). The working of the law in my historical existence is the reason, according to Bultmann, why I had a previous understanding of sin and forgiveness. "I must have had a previous understanding of sin and forgiveness if I am ever to understand what is being said to me."[9] But then for Bultmann this previous understanding can no longer be worked out by means of Kant's ethics, but must be arrived at through existential analysis. This, however, cannot finally describe the formal structure of moral actions.[10]

In addition to Barth,[11] Friedrich Gogarten was also more critical than Bultmann in speaking about the ethical basis of theology in Herrmann's thought. The manner in which—according to Herrmann—the power of morality in Jesus is to be perceived as "the only true God," Gogarten finds "remarkable."[12] Gogarten saw that in one respect Herrmann proceeded in exactly the same manner as his opponents. "He understands the 'historical' Jesus on the basis of a conception of Christ which he already had. The only difference is that it is for him not a metaphysical concept of Christ as it is for his opponents, but a concept thought out in terms of the idea of morality" (p. 381). But even Gogarten grants Herrmann that as the basis of our trust in Jesus "the incontrovertible reality of morality that confronts us in Jesus can quite rightly be taken into account" (p. 379). He does not, however, join Herrmann in finding the morality of Jesus in his exaltation, but with Luther he finds it in the "lowliness of Jesus" (p. 384) and then declares that "the history of Christ is ours, and our history is that of Christ" (p. 390). Thus Herrmann's ethicism is transformed into Gogarten's personalism.

In the writings of Bultmann and Gogarten, Herrmann's grounding of theology on ethics is at work subliminally, but it has recently appeared in much clearer form. In the writings of Ernst Fuchs it can at first glance appear to be a merely incidental turn of phrase when he speaks of the "ethical domination of our existence."[13] But even here we must be struck by the close relationship of this phraseology to the theological understanding of language as a liberating confrontation that is basic for Fuchs' thought.[14] The similarity to Herrmann is even clearer in the statement, "If the moral earnestness of the scholar is the existential condition for the interpretation of the New Testament, inasmuch as God's truth lays claim to the human conscience, then the search for the basis of human existence is the existentialist condition of such interpretation."[15] More recently Gerhard Ebeling's agreement with Herrmann is unmistakable when he says, "The only way in which theology can make itself understood in what it has to say is to seek out and confront humans in the ethical reality in which they find themselves." "That which is the real concern of theology—the gospel—can be expressed only in relation to law, because the gospel shows that it is gospel only in relation to law, that is, not by approaching the law as if it had no relationship to it, but by relating to it in a liberating manner."[16]

This last quotation from Ebeling illustrates the strength of this theological position. The ethical basis of theology in the school of Ritschl and especially its revival in Ebeling's work is regarded as the continuation of the Reformation doctrine of law and gospel. It was with good reason that he developed extensive portions of his position as the explication of the views of the young Luther. But Ebeling can appeal to others besides the Reformers and Herrmann.[17] Herrmann, with his ethical proof of theology, was by no means an innovator in the theological world of the nineteenth century. To a large degree his position corresponded to the manner in which the older supernaturalism had been based on Kant.[18] Above all, however, August G. Tholuck, the influential teacher not only of Ritschl and Herrmann but also of Martin Kähler, was influenced by the early-nineteenth-century "revival of religion" and presented the moral experience of mankind as the criterion of revelation. This experience was to resolve the moral discord that resulted from the experiencing of guilt: "If he (i.e., man) finds a revelation that is successful in resolving the discord in his inner being, then this is for him the true revelation."[19] On close inspection, we see that Ebeling's relationship to the Reformers' doctrine of law and gospel was mediated through this "revival theology" and its pietistic heritage. The view that the law which speaks in our conscience provides proof of the content of theological doctrines is not stated so pointedly by the Reformers, but was first asserted in the revival theology. Thus the program that Ebeling represents today is seen to be the expression of a quite specific theological tradition.

II

In 1878, a year before the publication of Herrmann's basic work in systematic theology, Nietzsche had already published his aphorisms of *Human, All-Too-Human*. In this book there is a chapter entitled "On the History of Moral Feelings," which expresses the basic ideas of the later works *Beyond Good and Evil* (1886) and *Toward a Genealogy of Morals* (1887). In his 1878 work Nietzsche was already challenging the general applicability of morality (Aphorism 96). The decisive feature for distinguishing between good and evil was "dependence on something traditional, law." Nietzsche continued: "It is of no importance how the tradition arose, but in any case it was without reference to good and evil or to some immanent categorical imperative, but primarily for the purpose of preserving a society, a people." The knowledge that "the entire realm of moral concepts is constantly in flux" led him beyond all fixed concepts of good and evil (Aphorism 56). According to Nietzsche, righteousness arose out of barter (Aphorism 92). Guilt, conscience, duty have their origin in commercial law.[20] A bad conscience is the result of the resentment felt by the oppressed,[21] and love that goes beyond what is just struck Nietzsche as stupid.[22]

While the individual explanations that Nietzsche gave are more or less one-sided, still the recognition of the historical relativity of ethics was established. Even if having a conscience is something inalienably human, the content of the conscience is subject to unpredictable transformations, which are closely connected with the changes in society and politics. The transformations of our social and political world, as well as the increasing conviction that the contents of the conscience vary, to which Nietzsche's writings contributed so greatly—all this helped bring about the crisis of ethics in which we find ourselves. To be sure, such a crisis could arise only because ethics had already cut itself off from its religious roots in the Christian tradition. The crisis of the Christian religion, which, among other points, was expressed in the establishment of the independence of ethics, is the basic cause of the ethical crisis through which we are living. The dissolution of traditional morality was already noticeable in the First World War. In the confusion of conscience during the time of National Socialism it gained in intensity to a degree that formerly was inconceivable. Only in the context of this crisis can we measure the weight of the decisions of conscience confronted by the men of July 20, 1944, whose memory we honor today. Today the relativity of ethical standards is unmistakable in the opposition of

Communist morality to that of the so-called Western nations, and in the struggle over atomic weapons the significance of ethical judgment is clear to everyone.

From here Wilhelm Herrmann's attempt to prove the truth of Christianity by the standard of the ethical consciousness appears in a ghostly light. Already in 1879, when he gave the basing of theology on moral consciousness its classic formulation, in terms of intellectual history the time was already past for such a concept in a comprehensive sense. The insights to which the future belonged had been expressed a year earlier by Nietzsche. In terms of intellectual history, Herrmann's efforts were out of date before they saw the light of day.

Consequently it is disturbing to find a contemporary theologian speaking of the "authority of the ethical" and commenting, in a revival of Herrmann's thought, that theology "can make itself understood only when it seeks for and encounters humans in the ethical reality in which they find themselves" (see note 16 of this chapter). Gerhard Ebeling, who advances this thesis, is thoroughly aware of the ethical crisis of the present day and makes specific reference to it.[23] How is it possible for him then to speak of the "authoriy of the ethical"? Ebeling finds in the life of humans together something that "constrains them to put things right." By awareness of this constraint we are drawn "into the realm, basic to ethical thought, of the distinction between good and evil."[24] At the high point of the development of his thought, Ebeling speaks of an "authority that is appropriate to the claims of those in need" (pp. 337f.). "The true stimulus to ethical reflection and the only one to be taken seriously is . . . our fellow human being who has suffered violence, who is constantly being humiliated and offended. . . . The response to this authoritative claim of our wronged fellow humans is commitment to righting the evil and the interpretation of this problem as a call to love one's neighbor" (p. 336). But is love for our neighbor the obvious response called for by our neighbor's plight? There are two reasons why I do not find this contention convincing. Both are closely connected with the question of the nature of love.

1. Even to discover the plight of those I encounter on my way through life requires an act of creative imagination. The imagination of love discovers the plight of our fellow humans in places where others see no plight at all, at least no plight that specifically requires their help. The plight of our fellow humans is therefore—to a frightening degree—hardly ever so obvious that it would be evident to everyone. In Luke 10, Jesus answers the question, "Who is my neighbor?" with the story of the good Samaritan, which concludes with the counterquestion, "Which of these three, do you think, proved neighbor to the man who fell among the robbers?" (Luke 10:36). Jesus took the question he was asked and turned it around; that is, a person is not our neighbor because we belong to a specific group of persons that includes him, but we become his neighbor through a free act of love. It is to such free acts of love which create neighbors that Jesus calls us when he says, "Go and do likewise."

2. Closely connected with the creative nature of love is the fact that the human situation outside the conventions of society cannot be directly interpreted as a "demand" upon us, and certainly not as a "radical" demand of selflessness as both Ebeling[25] and Knud E. Løgstrup contend.[26] A situation is never of itself clearly ethical; it is so only when confronted by a person who makes ethical decisions. Only the creative imagination of love discovers in a situation a need and at the same time the means for meeting it. The same situation, however, can give rise to quite different ethical responses. Thus we cannot say with Løgstrup, "The demands are completely contained in the concrete situation."[27] In any case, Christian ethics is the opposite of such situation ethics, because its starting point is not the situation but the creative imagination of love.[28] The person who is the object of love cannot make any demands on it but receives it as a gift. The elements of the situation are only the means by which love can bring something into being that was not previously there. No radical demand can be found in the

situation, or in or behind the fellow human being with whom I am involved,[29] but it is to be found in the activity of love itself, insofar as it contains the demand to give love scope and to search for opportunities where it can work. "Go and do likewise." Whatever the situation, the person who is full of love may regard it as an opportunity for expressing love. The light of love shines on him out of the situations of life, providing a lure and a challenge to express the love that is within him. But this always presupposes that the person is filled with love.

We must conclude that from a situation, even a situation where we recognize others as our fellow human beings, it is not possible to derive any universally valid authority of the ethical. Only those who live in the Christian tradition will be able to see in the love for humans as such the highest motive for conduct under all circumstances, whether the fellow human is Jew or non-Jew, worker or capitalist. For other viewpoints it makes a great difference in the evaluation of a situation what human group the person belongs to. This relativity of the contents of ethics cannot be overcome on the basis of ethics alone. Gruesome deeds are often performed with a subjectively good conscience. Therefore the relativity of ethics can be overcome only by more comprehensive approaches. Today no mere ethic is binding any longer. And an ethos can become binding only out of a total understanding of existence, insofar as it results in a specific ethical attitude that is meaningful. In contrast to Herrmann, Bultmann shows a consciousness of this when he attempts to find the approach to ethical questions in the framework of an existential analysis of human existence, but he remained all too restricted by his approach in terms of human subjectivity. An analogous attempt to move beyond the confines of the merely ethical is found in Fuchs and Ebeling in their theory of language, of the word-event, but it was too quickly narrowed to the opening up or restricting of existence, that is, to an ethical aspect in terms of the relationship between declaration and communication, which is characteristic for every historical language.[30] Løgstrup even expressly called for an ontological basis of morality.[31] If this is done, it should not once again be limited to an ontology of the ethical situation. The ontological question in the background of personal and ethical problems must, as Gerhard Gloege demanded in 1955, be framed in more comprehensive terms.[32] It is only out of each specific understanding of reality as a whole that the basic features of an ethical attitude emerge.

This also holds true for theology. Theology cannot expect to demonstrate the reality of its subject matter in terms of ethical relevance or of some presupposed ethical standard. On the contrary, the reality of God and of his revelation must first be firmly established if it is to have any ethical relevance at all, even though the ethical confirmation provided by those who believe in that reality can influence the public's verdict concerning the truth of the message. The Christian ethical conscience presupposes the truth of the Christian message. The "dogmatic proof" for which Herrmann was seeking must already be firmly established if we are to reach ethical conclusions. For Israel the authority of the law proclaimed at Sinai was based on the fact that the Lawgiver had already demonstrated his deity in the events of Israel's exodus from Egypt. Therefore the proclamation of Yahweh's law begins with the words, "I am the LORD your God, who brought you out of the land of Egypt, out of the house of bondage" (Ex. 20:2).[33] God's self-disclosure as he led Israel through history is the basis of the divine law. The case is similar for the New Testament. It is only knowledge of the love of the God who is revealed in Jesus Christ that frees us to express true love. In I John it says that if God has so loved us, that is, through the giving of his son as the expiation for our sins, then we are under obligation to love one another (I John 4:10-11). "We love, because he first loved us" (4:19). The question of the truth of what we say about God and about the revelation of his love in Jesus Christ must take precedence over the other question concerning the ethical relevance of the Christian message, and it cannot be narrowed *a priori* to that which already seems ethically significant.

Comprehensive knowledge of the reality of God, of the specific reality of the created world, and of our existence is the only possible basis for understanding the extent to which the ethical consequences we draw from that knowledge are applicable.

The apostle Paul appealed to an implicit knowledge that even the heathen had of law, but this was not the way in which he presented to the heathen the deity of the God whom he was proclaiming. Instead, in the course of the development of the thought of the letter to the Romans he had already called attention to a special, though equally implicit, knowledge that the Gentiles had of God (Rom. 1:19ff.).[34] And in what follows he made use of points of view that, in terms of the issues we are discussing here, belong to the realm of an ontology of mankind (Romans 5). The thesis that a dogmatic proof must be concentrated on moral conscience finds no support in Paul.

Can this thesis appeal to the Reformers? There is no question but that the dialectic of law and gospel constituted the basic issue of the Reformation, and it must also be conceded that the good news of the forgiveness of sins presupposes the law. But this theme of the Reformation presupposes the framework of a still undisputed Christian tradition, and the unquestioned validity of the biblical statements about the actions of God. Only on the basis of a *notitia historiae* that on the whole was still unquestioned can we understand in its historic setting the Reformers' emphasis on the insufficiency of a merely historic knowledge for salvation, on God's promise as the final cause of history (*Apology of the Augsburg Confession* IV, 51), and on faith as the fulfillment of the law. To derive the dogmatic proof of the reality of God and his revelation from the verification of the gospel by the law, as Herrmann wanted to do, is far removed from the thought of the Reformation. In the sixteenth century there was no necessity for anything of the sort, because the reality of God, to which the Bible bore witness, and the history of his revelation in Israel and in Jesus Christ, was still the undisputed presupposition for the real theme of the Reformation.

If we keep this in mind, it is clear how different our present-day intellectual situation is from that of the Reformation. In the modern period the reality of God itself and of the traditional understanding of biblical history has been called into question. The questions this raises can no longer be overpowered with a false sense of authority by employing the Reformation dialectic of law and gospel. They demand new approaches and solutions. The attempt to force the modern discussion of the reality of God and of the history of revelation to which the Bible bears witness into an ethical-existential schema in analogy to that of law and gospel, is, instead, characteristic of the "revival theology" and of Wilhelm Herrmann's systematic theology and its recent successors. Quite apart from the unavoidable abbreviation of the theme of theology (which did not start with Bultmann and Ebeling, but is in the last analysis the consequence of the way the pietistic ancestors of "revival theology" restricted their interests to the ethical), any attempt to prove the truth of dogmatics by ethical experience, as was Herrmann's goal, is in itself doomed to failure, because, as we have seen, such a program has been outmoded by the advances in intellectual history. The question of the reality of God and of his revelation must be posed for its own sake and in the interest of ethics as well. Only when the reality of God and of his revelation is firmly established can life be lived in accordance with it. Only if we first confront in complete earnestness and openness the question of the reality of God and his revelation, can we maintain access to that realm of problems in which the Reformation issues of law and gospel first arose. But if theology seeks to use the basic concepts of the sixteenth century in order to overcome the questions framed so differently in our present situation, the only result will be that theology bypasses today's reality and questions and attains illusory solutions.

In the present ethical crisis the world is expecting help from the Christian tradition, from the Christian church. If theology has a contribution to make, it will not be in the form of an ethical foundation for Christian truth, but on the contrary in a new theological basis for ethics. It is not enough to have individual statements by theologians on this or that ethical question. If theology once again succeeds in permeating and understanding the whole of our reality from the point of view of the Christian tradition, and in coming to terms with it while maintaining the power of the reality of the God of whom it speaks, then out of such an understanding of our reality will grow the power of that love which is able to solve the moral dilemma of the present day.

4

AN ANSWER TO GERHARD EBELING[1]

Munich, September 29, 1972

Dear Mr. Ebeling,

For many reasons the letter I intended to write you, setting forth my position regarding your answer to my inaugural address in Mainz on the crisis in ethics, has been long delayed. One reason was that in my repeated readings of your answer I felt more and more that our conversations in the preceding year had produced a considerably higher degree of understanding of one another's positions, if not of agreement. Nevertheless I do not want to fail to discuss your arguments.

In your evaluation of the present crisis in ethics, you specified your ideas concerning the self-evident authority of the ethical in a manner that, it seems to me, represents an advance, and a narrowing of the differences between our positions. You rightly designate as the "threatening factor" of the present crisis of ethical consciousness the fact that not only is the validity of individual norms shattered but "the phenomenon of the ethical itself is obscured, reduced to certain conventions and game rules, to 'traffic regulations' in the broad sense, whose binding force is dependent on considerations of expediency and police surveillance."[2] I can agree with this description of the situation. But it does seem to me that the matter which you have described in this way is not simply a consequence of "technological thought." In the period between the two World

Wars, and even after the last war, the belief was widespread that there was in principle an antagonism between personality and technology. This seems to me highly questionable. It represents an ideology of withdrawal from a society revolutionized by technology into an individuality which lacks roots in society, but which does still fulfill a social function, albeit a rather questionable one. I am aware only of certain concrete expressions of personality in relationship to various ways of employing technical possibilities and means, but not of any opposition in principle between technology and personality as such. Therefore I cannot follow your characterizing of the ethical crisis (which you previously described so accurately), as the expression of a "mechanization of human relationships and even of the relationship of man to himself." Instead of that, I see this phenomenon in the context of the critique of traditional moral norms, as conducted by Nietzsche in especially telling fashion. Of course in terms of intellectual history, the present ethical crisis cannot simply be traced to Nietzsche. It is necessary, however, to explain the great extent of his influence. Anyone who attempts this must take into consideration the fact that at the decisive point—that is, the reduction of moral norms to human values by Nietzsche and other interpreters of morality such as Mill and, not least, Freud—there were articulated possibilities and tendencies that have their roots in modern political history, specifically in the emancipation of politics and ethics from religion after the period of religious wars.

As you yourself emphasize,[3] ethics as such must be distinguished from the validity of individual ethical norms. The phenomenon of the ethical as a search for the Good or for the identity of the self was threatened because specific norms adhered to by other persons or in another time have been rejected. That is of course "part of the phenomenon of the ethical."[4] But the situation looks quite different when all norms whatever are regarded as the expression of arbitrary subjectivity, or as being established by special interests. Such a radical critique of norms casts doubt on ethical consciousness itself. Our awareness of moral obligations inevitably becomes vague when it can no longer be clarified in terms of any indisputable, universally valid norm, because all norms are suspected of being based on rules that serve special interests. The same holds true for a consciousness of guilt. Neither the consciousness of guilt nor that of ethical responsibility has simply disappeared in the present crisis of the ethical. It seems to me, as to you, that it is not possible for such fundamental anthropological phenomena to disappear. This could come about only through far-reaching changes in human nature, spread out over a long evolutionary process. I believe that the present crisis of ethical consciousness is characterized by confusion and by our limited ability to identify any content for the experience of guilt or of moral obligation. This confusion, however, is clearly related to the universally problematic state of moral norms. This results in superficial observance, inability to resist the pressure to conform to general behavior patterns, and in brief, everything that you designate as the "reduction" of ethical norms to "traffic regulations," toward which we do not feel any real inner compulsion to conform.

In the light of this situation it is difficult for me to understand how it is possible to justify the assertion of an "authority" of the ethical, even when I take into account the fact that you are not thinking of an "authority that is directly recognizable and immediately obvious."[5] It seems more plausible to me that, as you write in your reply,[6] the "problem" of the ethical cannot simply be "shoved aside," if by this you intended to say that the phenomenon is problematic in itself and not merely for our investigation of it.[7] In this sense I can also agree with your identification of "factors that compel us to understand" the ethical problem. But it does appear to me that in your discussion of the "impulse to commitment,"[8] and especially of the "impulse to get things right,"[9] your formal analysis of human behavior unexpectedly slips over into a demand for commitment and "making amends" in the sense of love for one's neighbor. To my way of looking at it, this does not deal adequately with the complexity of the issues. The basic experience of resistance against evil, to which you appeal, presupposes, in my opinion, an idea of the Good that is strong enough to lead to the formation of community and that is given concrete expression in resistance to evil. If we explore the effectiveness of the idea of the Good, we end up—as Platonic philosophy demonstrates in classic manner—in the realm of metaphysics, and finally that of religion. Such a course might make it possible, if anything can, to establish a basis for ethics.[10] But the realm of ethics could then no longer be regarded as an autonomous phenomenon, independent of religion and metaphysics; it would be firmly embedded in our understanding of reality. If we ignore this, and especially the religious and metaphysical implications of the experience of reality, then there remains of the "impulse to set things right" little more than the tendency to pass moral judgment on the conduct of others. In any case this tendency does not seem to have been appreciably influenced by the present uncertainty over moral norms. It seems to represent primarily a psychological need that does not appear to be disturbed from another perspective, nor does it guarantee that the person making the judgment will abide by the rules on which the judgment is based instead of providing generous exceptions for his own behavior. This illustrates the relativity of ethical norms, to the point of complete arbitrariness. It is the result of divorcing ethical discussion from the religious and metaphysical implications of our experience of reality, because in this way all norms for conduct are made dependent on the values that people establish, and there is no other source for these norms.

In view of this confused situation, I cannot speak of any "authority" of ethics, because the expression "authority" demands a clarity in the orientation of the conscience that is lacking here. For the understanding of law in the Reformation as well as for the various forms of ethical interpretation of the Christian faith in Rationalism and in the piety of the period of the Enlightenment there is, however, such authority, even for the contents of the norms. When we speak of the "authority" of the ethical, the phenomenon of the ethical as such cannot be separated from the necessity that ethical norms have content. And vice versa, the relativizing of not one ethical norm or the other, but of all such norms to where they are more or less arbitrary values, leads to an obscuring of the ethical as such, even though it does lead to private goals and to the construction of artificial formulations, comparable to traffic regulations as guides for social conduct.

Scheler's and Hartmann's philosophical ethic of values recognized the ruinous consequences that Nietzsche's critique of norms had for ethical consciousness, and thus they concerned themselves with trying to show that values existed prior to all human assigning of values. The problem with these attempts lay in the assumption of an ideal sphere of values which differ from and are independent of empirical reality, and which only "adhere to" the given empirical values. Nevertheless the collapse of the ethic of values because of the inconcinnity of the relationship of value to being demonstrates the priority of the ontological problem and the vital significance of an understanding of reality for every attempt to establish a basis for ethics. This state of affairs reveals itself on another plane in the dependence of ethical convictions on the world view existing at a particular time.

My critique of the thesis of the "authority" of the ethical was concerned with the primacy of our understanding of reality for the task of providing a basis for ethics. I believe that this thesis echoes the conviction (so influential in modern thought) of the autonomy of the ethical consciousness, especially its independence of religion and metaphysics. But now in your essay on the "Authority of the Ethical" there is the statement: "Even a neutral analysis of the ethical problem would confirm that at its heart lies the question, 'What is man?' and in one way or another it builds on the assumptions of a specific world view and shares in its questionable nature."[11] I cannot disagree with this statement. My critique of the further arguments of your essay can then be formulated as follows: You did not follow up on the nature of the problem as you yourself characterized it in that statement. You based your argument on the "priority" of the ethical, the "precedence of what is at hand, concrete, and attainable" when we confront the unavoidable nature of ethical decisions. I am not at all closed to this point of view, but what is involved here is a practical priority for action, not the argument that an ethical phenomenon can be isolated in a theoretical analysis. That which is "at hand" and "urgent" is by no means conclusive for ethical reflection, as your combining of "at hand and conclusive" on the next page seems to assume.[12]

When I emphasize, in the same sense as your own statement quoted above, the primacy of our understanding of reality for the analysis of ethical phenomena and for the basis of ethical norms, it is not in order to provide a "new basis for a specifically Christian ethic," as you claim in your response.[13] I do it because the ethical as a "common concern of all mankind"[14] cannot be isolated and made autonomous in contrast to the living context of the human experience of reality and meaning.[15] This is also the point of my critique of Wilhelm Herrmann, to which I will return later. In any case, I have difficulty with your distinction between the ethical problem "in its full breadth" and that "which concerns only the Christian and is true and obligatory only under the presupposition of the Christian faith."[16] Is then the Christian faith only of limited interest, relevant only for those who profess it, and not for everyone? I believe that you and I are agreed that the Christian faith involves that which is common to all mankind. Therefore I could not take that as my theme while leaving the Christian faith out of account. Instead, as I understand the matter, the point to be discussed in theology is the extent to which the Christian tradition can cast light on the common human concern of how we are to understand reality and then also the issue of how our ethical actions are to be oriented. This is your contribution to the general discussion.

This means that the discussion of the experience of meaning and the religious discussion closely connected with it, including the question of the reality of God, is, in spite of its being keenly disputed, just as much a concern of all mankind as is the phenomenon of the ethical, in reference to which the various specific orientations to the world are today just as much in dispute. The position that the authority of ethics for all mankind distinguishes it from the religious question, which is to be left to the private sphere, was characteristic of the early modern period. At that time, in the face of the insurmountable divisions among Christian groups, people were seeking for a new basis for human life in community and believed they had discovered it in basic ethical insights.[17] In this view the acceptance of the authority of such insights was combined with the thesis of the autonomy of ethics over against religion and metaphysics. However, when ethical principles came to be regarded as rules established by a value-creating will, which can be changed if that same will wishes them changed, the earlier conviction became untenable. This new view is not arbitrary but is the inevitable consequence of cutting loose from metaphysical and religious convictions, which until then had been the unspoken basis of the claim to ethical authority. What else then besides the will of man himself stands behind the authority of ethical values, if all religious and metaphysical faith has disappeared? And the will of man means those mutually hostile values and directions of the will. Here it is obvious that the independence of ethics from religion and metaphysics was an illusion that could be maintained only as long as certain elements of the common basis of the warring conceptions of Christianity, which the Enlightenment brought together under the theme "natural religion," were not under attack. Today the ethical is just as much in dispute as religion and metaphysics are, so that it is no longer available as an alternative basis for that which is common to all mankind. In this situation it is by no means necessary to "capitulate."[18] Still it must be granted that today in all spheres, and not least of all in aesthetics, there is disagreement about what is common to all mankind. This disagreement involves us all, and out of it what is common to mankind must be determined anew. This is what distinguishes our present situation from that of the early modern period, when a still undisputed agreement in ethics could be taken for granted in contrast to the hopelessly fragmented state of the sectarian formulations of the religious consciousness.

If the thesis of the independence of ethics is recognized as a historical stage in the process of the dissolution of Christian and metaphysical certainty, it makes little sense to reestablish that position and then try to base theology on it. This is why the viability of Herrmann's position seems so doubtful to me. Herrmann explicitly attempted to base theology and religion on the phenomenon of the ethical, which he believed to be independent of all theoretical consciousness and also of all metaphysics. In order to describe this matter more precisely, it would be necessary to discuss Herrmann's development in more detail than I did in my inaugural address in Mainz. This development led him away from his original intention of finding an ethical "proof" for the universal validity of Christianity[19] and into stressing the subjectivity of moral experience itself. Nevertheless the dualism of theoretical knowledge of the world and moral-religious experience was not overcome, as far as I can tell, by the development in Herrmann's thought. In any case, I cannot find in Herrmann's assertion that ethical experience as such includes a relationship to the world[20] any overcoming or modification of this dualism. As I have earlier pointed out, Herrmann's position that religion and ethics belong together in contrast to knowledge of the world does not exclude their being separated in other contexts, but Herrmann placed great weight on the independence of religious experience, "in contrast to Kant."[21] Consequently I cannot help being surprised at your observation that I had "completely obscured"[22] this difference. For Herrmann, as was the case earlier for the old supernatural theology, the religious element was not simply an expression of ethical consciousness, or a consequence of it, but was a supplement, something independent that was added to it. It did, however, still have its human relevance and truth, but only through its relevance to the ethical problems of life, as the solution of ethical dilemmas, especially the experience of guilt. It is in this sense that I find in Herrmann's thought an attempt to provide an ethical basis for theology.

You and I hold differing interpretations of Herrmann in connection with the relationship which he says religion holds to ethics on the one hand and to knowledge of the world on the other (which in spite of your discussion of this point[23] I continue to regard as an ethicistic simplification). In this connection I am not at all convinced by your assurance that, "in reference to the necessity of a breakthrough to the ontological question and the insufficiency of a purely ethical or purely personal manner of looking at the issue, there is no quarrel between us."[24] It would be nice if that were the case, but I have the impression that it is here that the decisive point in dispute is to be found. Perhaps the intention expressed in your statement would make it possible to clarify and overcome the difference. But that even here we are not always in agreement can be seen in your next statement. You say that, "in the continuing attempt to establish the truth of God and his revelation," I am "not willing to acknowledge that realm of truth which is characterized by human involvement."[25] I could limit my answer to quoting those among my critics who charge that it is because my arguments take anthropology as their starting point, especially in the question of God and of Christology, that I miss the mark of what constitutes theology. In this respect I feel that I share with you the modern focus of the themes of theology on understanding mankind. What is the point then of your reprimand? It makes sense only if, as seems to be the case, you see "human involvement" only when theology is concerned with the ethical issues of life. Here the difference mentioned above is clear. For me "human involvement" means first of all a concern with the problem of the meaning of human involvement in history and human self-experience. Ethics seems to me to be only one aspect of this comprehensive theme. This is true also of the "will to truth," which you mention at the conclusion of your reply in reference to the ethical basis of knowledge. All commitment to truth is preceded not only by a prior knowledge of truth and error but also by an acquaintance with truth that produces knowledge, so that in this way a "methodical knowledge of truth" is possible, if at all.

Any direct ethical "human involvement" that is not mediated by an understanding of the content and meaning of the world, and thus by concrete experience of it, would rob ethical decisions of the nature of free insight. By thus emphasizing the priority of the question of meaning I intend to recognize the interests of the ethical consciousness as an awareness of freedom. Freedom depends on the communication of ethical relevance through an understanding of meaning, because it brings with it the possibility of forming one's own judgment.

"Human involvement" demands above all an experience of meaning and meaningful contexts—that is, the dimension of significance. But this is not to say that that involvement is "independent of the experience of one's conscience."[26] What we know through the conscience is also one form of what we experience of meaning, an excellent form insofar as it involves—as you have described in impressive manner—the totality of one's own existence. Yet the specific meaning of what we experience through the conscience is valid only when its distinctive nature is honored in the more comprehensive context of the question of meaning. When it is isolated, the appeal to the conscience has, in the light of the present-day uncertainty of conscience concerning moral norms, only a subjective authority. Even in the self-consciousness of the individual, the voice of conscience by itself is open to the suspicion that it is giving expression only to the voice of the superego. But what the conscience itself really is before such functions take place can be best established in the context of the question of meaning. This is precisely what you did not do in your essay on this topic when you related conscience to the consciousness of the whole of reality,[27] and thus to the "context of man, world, and God."[28] I had the same state of affairs in mind when I termed the conscience the existential relevance of reason, though there was a quite specific understanding of "reason" behind my statement.

After having said all this, there is no need for me to discuss your clever surmise that I am "concerned to establish a verification of our statements about God . . . that would be independent of the experience of conscience."[29] I term this surmise "clever," because in a conversation with a theologian it has *a priori* a high degree of improbability. A similar response could be made to your surmise on the following page that I am aiming "to establish the truth of the Christian proclamation prior to and outside of the situation of faith."[30] Your assumption would have been nearer the mark if you had said that in my understanding of the situation of faith there is a difference between us. That is, for me this situation is not determined directly and exclusively by the ethical dimension, but by the context of the experience of meaning that includes our experience of the world, by the explication of the meaning of that experience, and by the concerns of ethics.

In my opposition to the isolation of ethical discussion, I hold that our understanding of reality should take precedence over the consciousness of ethical norms. Your response touches on this thesis only in that your ascribe to me a concern to create a "correspondence" to a long-outmoded *"fides historica,"* which is intended to present "an unassailable assurance of the reality of God and of the biblical view of history."[31] Anyone who reads your response will have difficulty avoiding the impression that such an attempt is eccentric and anachronistic, especially because the formulation you cite arouses the impression that the astonishing author whom you are debating has until now been unaware of the provisional nature of all present knowledge and the pluralism that has resulted from this state of affairs, as well as the demolishing of "the biblical view of history" by historical criticism. The reader will not know that I mentioned the *notitia historiae* of the Reformers only as one historical example among others of the priority which our understanding of reality has over the issues of ethics, and that this understanding includes ethical issues. At the same time you modify the statement that the Reformers really presupposed such an unassailable *notitia historiae* when you concede to me that I surely know that "this presupposition, which is no longer valid today, cannot be revived."[32] The fact that the Reformers' statements about faith were based on this presupposition does mean that the divorce of the experience of the conscience and of the ethical description of the "situation of faith" from this presupposition would involve a substantial distortion of the theme of the Reformation, especially if their presupposition is no longer tenable for us.

When the Reformers' application of biblical history to the questions of repentance and conscience was made independent of that presupposition, it became necessary that liberation from the ethical dilemma should then serve as the guarantee of the content of the Christian tradition, including even the factual nature of the event of salvation. As I stated in my lecture in Mainz, this constituted the pietistic reformulation of the Reformation theology of faith, and it was carried out on the basis of that isolation of the ethical realm which I was criticizing. I am as little concerned as you are with trying to repristinate Reformation positions such as the *notitia historiae,* because it was based on a precritical concept of authority that we can no longer share. It is no longer possible in this area or in any other to deal adequately with the different set of problems we confront today simply by appealing to the formulations of the Reformation. Neither am I concerned therefore to "create" a "correspondence" to that *notitia historiae* in the sense of an analogical application of it. As I have clearly said, I used that idea only as one historical example among others for the present-day problem of the precedence of our understanding of reality over the issues of ethics, which can be discussed only within the context of that understanding.

When the question is raised of what contribution the Christian faith can make to the solution of our present ethical crisis, the first step toward an answer is to set forth the understanding of reality which the Christian faith implies in the context of the contemporary experience of reality. This is a contribution to the understanding of that experience. Here then a confrontation with the theme of history becomes unavoidable, not as something that is specifically Christian and nothing more, but as a theme basic to the modern self-understanding of man. Yet it is characteristic of Christianity in a special way, because for some two thousand years Christianity has clung to the historic figure of Jesus, and because the God of the Bible is a God of history. This does not imply the adoption of a biblical view of history, but it does make it possible to bring the modern issues of our historical consciousness into touch with its historical source, the biblical understanding of God. It is thus not possible to claim that I am concerned with "an unassailable assurance . . . of the biblical view of history."[33]

If this was not already clear, it should have become clear through my renunciation of a view of theological history in terms of promise and fulfillment in favor of the concept of tradition history, a step regretted by those on the side opposite to yours. Furthermore, there are no "unassailable verifications" in questions of history, a point I have stressed. This, however, does not alter the fact that in this area the highest possible degree of certainty is to be found in history's judgment of probability, to which no other sources of certainty are superior. At the conclusion of my article "Toward a Theology of the History of Religion,"[34] I believe I made it sufficiently clear that even in reference to the reality of God there can be no "unassailable verifications," so that I need not go into the matter further. I will only remind the reader of the point of view which I developed there, that the question of the reality of God—whether God is real and if so, how—involves the openness of history. Thus even this question points once more to the theme of history. Its specifically Christian relevance is given on the one hand by the connection of Christian faith with the historical figure of Jesus, and on the other through the special relationship of the biblical God to the experience of reality as history, so that these two aspects are closely related. Only because the biblical God is the God of history can the meaning of the historical Jesus become the theological theme for the present day in the context of the history of the transmission of Christianity, and not merely a topic in the history of culture.

You might not object that even a contemporary investigation of the meaning of the historical Jesus, first in his own historical context and then in the framework of the application of history in general, would not progress beyond the limits of the Reformation concept of the *notitia historiae*, even though this concept has been judged unsatisfactory and the distinction has been drawn between it and saving faith. As you see it, the final point for discussion between us is "how the *fides iustificans* arises out of the *fides historica*."[35] I frame the question of the significance of the historical Jesus in the context of the modern discussion of the philosophy of history, specifically the analysis of historical experience as developed by Dilthey, but in opposition to a positivistic history that separates fact and meaning. This differs from the Reformation *notitia historiae* in that it does not exclude the question of the meaning of historical data, but even has it as its specific theme, and in that this is the only way in which a concept of history in its entirety becomes possible.

For Melanchthon the limitation of the *notitia historiae* was that it could provide only a superficial view of history, because it ignored the *causa finalis*, which is the truly constitutive element of this history, and which for Melanchthon was identical with the forgiveness of sins (*Apology of the Augsburg Confession* IV, 51). The final cause is thus salvation, and it can be grasped only on the basis of belief in God's promises. In this connection it may be said that any history, if it is not artificially isolated from the system of meaning that characterizes it, reaches out in its own way, according to its own significance, lays hold on the interpreter of history, and draws him into its system of meaning, the ultimate extent of which is the totality of history, in which the reflective observer of history knows himself to be involved. Objective knowledge of history does not exclude the possibility of becoming involved in the content of history itself, however much the demand for objectivity stresses the distinction between the content and the subjective presuppositions of the interpreter. Nor does objectivity consist, as has been foolishly contended, in distancing oneself from content. It consists in a passionate involvement with the content, through which the one who asks the correct questions overcomes the subjective limitations that separate him from the matter at hand. However, insofar as transcending oneself through involvement is the essence of subjectivity, a true relationship to the content (that is, objectivity) is the expression of the highest subjectivity. Such a true relationship includes the consciousness that the meaning of past events, insofar as they extend into the still-open future, cannot be grasped by mere contemplation. This can happen only through anticipation of the future, an act of trusting the meaning, the content of which depends on the verification of the tradition by the present experience of the interpreter. This state of affairs is central for historical understanding, because what is transmitted as history is always dependent on language, on words, in which the actors and transmitters themselves have anticipated ultimate truth, and thus have reached out beyond the present time of the interpreter into the future that, even for him, is still open. This always involves salvation, and not solely in the Christian tradition. Such salvation is not to be explained in ethical categories only; indeed, it has as its content the positive fulfillment of the meaning of one's own existence in the context of all that is real. The Christian belief in salvation comes into play wherever people let themselves be involved in the meaning which the history of Jesus has for salvation; this history verifies itself for them as the fulfillment of the meaning of their present situation through their present experience. I doubt whether this meaning of salvation can still be made directly understandable today by the old concepts of justification and the forgiveness of sins, since the moralistic and legalistic connotations of these concepts have obscured their universal validity as far as anyone oriented to the question of the meaning of reality is concerned. For this reason we need to interpret these traditional expressions if we are to make it clear that they deal with the possibility of having fellowship with God.

It should be possible for us to agree that in history as the history of human beings the issue is that of verifying or not verifying verbally articulated anticipations of ultimate truth and ultimate salvation. I believe that I am in agreement with you in the insight that such anticipation of that which is not at present accessible can be made possible only through language. Consequently, these three things belong closely to each other: the inaccessible reality of God, language, and history. How to describe this relationship more precisely is the real issue of our conversation with each other. What you have portrayed as the hermeneutical process of the word-event, and what I designate as the history of the transmission of traditions, are ultimately not two distinct themes, but different attempts to come closer to a solution of one and the same problem. That we share a common theme would become even clearer if you did not explain the concept of the word-event exclusively in terms of the ethical question of events between persons but would include in your analyses the relationship of language to reality, a question that stands in the foreground of the philosophy of language—just as I, on the other hand, endeavor to express in the discussion of history the meaning of human speech for historical experience, and with it also your concern with the question of salvation.

With warm greetings, I remain, yours,

Wolfhart Pannenberg

5

THE BASIS OF ETHICS
IN THE THOUGHT OF ERNST TROELTSCH

Among the Christian theologians of this century who were concerned with preventing the Christian religion and Christian theology from wandering down sectarian byways, out of touch with the general development of culture, Ernst Troeltsch is today the outstanding figure. Through his works in intellectual and social history, theology made a contribution at the forefront of the confrontation with the problems of the age. Troeltsch related Christianity and Christian theology to the modern context with a perceptivity and insight that have not been surpassed. His formulations of the problems and tasks with which he confronted Christian thought have not lost their validity and their capacity for clarifying issues, even though (or perhaps because) the epoch that followed Troeltsch was concerned with dialectical theology and its consequences and believed it was necessary to follow another path. Even the direction that they took was, as we shall see, anticipated by Troeltsch. Dialectical theology, however, pursued it with a one-sided devotion against which Troeltsch could have warned it ahead of time.

In the context of his theory of the modern world and his concomitant "research in methodology and philosophy of religion," a basis "on which a Christian doctrine of faith and life can finally begin to take shape," Troeltsch's interest as he wrote in 1912 in the foreword to his *Soziallehren der christlichen Kirchen und Gruppen* ("Social Teachings of the Christian

Churches and Groups") shifted "in its major emphasis toward ethics." In terms of early Protestantism, which Troeltsch had dealt with in his earliest work, this was more of a shift than it was in terms of the theology of Ritschl, his own starting point. Indeed that theology had stressed the issues of ethics as basic for Christian doctrine. Troeltsch continued this emphasis in a consistent and also much more comprehensive manner by tracing his theory of history back to an ethical "metaphysics" of human behavior. In this way he succeeded in including in ethical discussion a theme that since the time of Kant and the discussions of rationalism and supernaturalism had struggled against being subordinated to an *a priori* ethic. He accomplished this, however, only by expanding ethics into a general philosophy of culture and society. To do this, Troeltsch drew on Schleiermacher's ethics in opposition to those of Kant. But while Schleiermacher worked with an abstraction of reality instead of empirical history, Troeltsch included the philosophy of history within ethics, and by so doing he was able to provide an ethical basis for all the issues of Christian theology. But because Troeltsch employed his ethical approach in so comprehensive a manner, he was also carrying it to its limits. The insight of the dialectical theologians in this matter gave legitimacy to the way in which they reversed Troeltsch's priority of ethics over dogmatics, in spite of all the criticism of the inadequate manner in which they carried out this reversal.

The publication of Wilhelm Herrmann's *Ethik* in 1901 led Troeltsch to give a comprehensive presentation of his view of the problem of providing a basis for ethics. His major contribution, "Grundprobleme der Ethik, erörtert aus Anlass von Herrmanns Ethik" ("Basic Problems of Ethics Viewed in the Light of Herrmann's Ethics"), which first appeared in 1902 in the journal *Zeitschrift für Theologie und Kirche*,[1] set forth his disagreements with Herrmann and at the same time sketched his own ethical position.

Troeltsch agrees with Herrmann in the assumption that ethics, "as the study of the ultimate goals and purposes of human existence,"[2] "is the supreme and most fundamental intellectual discipline, and the study of religion must fit within its framework."[3] Troeltsch saw in this the expression of a specifically modern development. In premodern Christianity, including early Protestantism, "ethics still belonged to the realm of the subjective and of practical application, while religion belonged to the only objective realm, that of authoritative revelation."[4] In the modern period, however, this relationship was reversed. Ethics, now independent of dogmatics and in opposition to it, became the universally valid intellectual discipline concerned with the practical themes of human life, while dogmatics was discredited by denominational narrowness and antagonisms. As a result there could now be an attempt "to reconstruct a badly shaken dogmatics on the basis of ethics."[5] Troeltsch came more and more to identify this decisive change with the Neo-Calvinism of the English Puritans and Independents of the seventeenth century.[6] Here the combination of Calvinistic motifs with motifs from spiritual and Anabaptist sources led these movements to deduce from the Reformation principle of Christian freedom the rights of individuals to enjoy civic freedom, and, by adoption of the Stoic "absolute" natural law, to replace the unified denominational state with the principle of religious freedom and of "free" churches. The distinctive nature of particular religious confessions was placed in the context of a conception of natural law motivated by Christian principles, and this is in accord with the precedence which ethics won over dogmatics through the influence of Neo-Calvinism.

According to Troeltsch, the theoretical basis of an independent ethic and the corresponding interpretation of religion as "an essentially practical attitude of the human spirit" and "as a support for and strength of morality" culminated in the practical philosophy of Kant.[7] Nevertheless he held that it was necessary to "supplement the Kantian ethic."[8] He agreed with Kant that ethics rests "on *a priori* thought that results in experience" (ibid.). He preferred, however, to understand this basic thought in the sense of an establishing of goals through reason, rather than in the form of a "mere concept of law." Thus there developed out of "ideally necessary ends" the distinction between individual goals and social goals, and from this the individual morality of personal character development and social morality, "which presuppose each other and mutually determine each other."[9] In Kant, according to Troeltsch, there developed "under the constraint of the parallels to theoretical transcendentalism" a concentration of ethical analysis on the subject. If one were to follow this approach, the result would be that "the concept of morality would include exclusively subjective ends and goals, . . . which concern the relationship of the subject to itself and to the analogical relationships of others to it, and it would be totally impossible that even objective ends could partake of the nature of objective, formal necessity."[10]

It is not possible to accept this critique without further reflection. Even Troeltsch was aware that Kant, on the basis of his ethics, could develop a concept of the state and a philosophy of history. At first glance this fact contradicts the observation that starting with Kant's ethics it is possible to arrive only at the establishment of subjective ends. Of course it cannot be denied that the transcendental questions which Kant raised actually sought to find the basis of ethics exclusively in subjectivity. In this, however, it was not merely the objective ends of social institutions that were subordinated to the concept of universal law, but all ends and goals whatever. This subordination of the concept of ends to the formal point of view of the universal validity of the law is probably responsible for the fact that the objective ends incorporated in social institutions in Kant's ethics do not have the fundamental importance that Troeltsch wished to ascribe to them. Insofar as the moral law is first applied to the subjective ends and goals of the individual and only secondarily to social ends, we cannot deny that there is an element of truth in Troeltsch's critique of Kant. But it would certainly have been more convincing if he had concentrated his criticism on the formal nature of Kant's concept of absolute universal validity and contrasted it with the concept of ends as the starting point for establishing the basis of ethics, instead of making the allegedly one-sided preference of subjective ends and goals the center of his line of argument. The consequence of this confusion was that Troeltsch regarded his own teleological basis of ethics with its stress on objective social goals alongside the subjective goals of a personal ethic as a mere "supplement" to the ethics of Kant. In reality this involved a totally new approach. Troeltsch underestimated the difficulty of establishing a new basis of this sort, because he thought it involved merely a "supplementing" of the "subjective" ethics of Kant by Schleiermacher's "objective" ethic of values.[11] The consequences of this inadequate reflection on basic issues will be seen later on in this essay. Troeltsch's interpretation of Kant's ethics as limited to subjective ends is hard to define and may be explained in part by his line of argument against the ethics of Herrmann, which can truly be characterized as an ethic of subjective ends. Its starting point is the human striving for self-assertion, toward which our wills are set. Herrmann states that this goal can be attained only if our personal life attains unity by a unified will, which results from subordinating our lives to a unified goal. This is not thought of, however, as the highest good. The argument shifts abruptly from consideration of the question of a goal that gives unity to our life to consideration of the reality of morality in other persons who are therefore authoritative for us. The question thus becomes one of a concept of moral law that as "absolute obligation" provides the basis for the unity of the person, a unity that is already real in those others, and for which we are seeking.[12] In this way the Kantian ethic of law is incorporated into an ethic of personality, which leads again from the concept of law back into the realm of the subjectivity of life. The leitmotif of this subjectivity is the thought of moral independence. Troeltsch rightly noted that here there was no appropriate recognition of the ethical relevance of social institutions. Even in the later editions of

Herrmann's *Ethik*, social institutions are regarded only as naturally developing human societies in which ethical actions are carried out. "The ethical values of marriage, the state, society, science, and art, all these are never considered by Herrmann as ethical ends or values, but merely as forms of society that are the result of natural drives."[13]

Troeltsch notes with approval that in Herrmann's thought a results ethic occupies the foreground, not an ethic based on law. This point of view should have received even more stress, and the entire system of concepts should be developed out of the ideally necessary results, with their division into individual and social goals.[14] Instead of this, however, he felt Herrmann adapted his thought to "Kant's much disputed idea" of the purely formal or categorical nature of ethical goals.[15] Thus for him the essence of Christian ethics consisted only in the "attainment of the strength to be autonomous," so that in reference to the "relationship to the world" as well as for "the development of a specifically Christian morality . . . nothing remains" to be done "except to make it possible for this formal concept of the good to be realized only in Christianity."[16] If we abandon Christian claims to exclusivity which, in spite of the universal applicability of morality, deny that it can be realized outside Christianity, then we are taking our stand with Fichte and Kant. "They meant what they said when from these presuppositions they arrived at a Christian ethic that was superior only in degree." In Herrmann's thought as well, "the specifically Christian element of Christian ethics . . . does not consist in any concrete expressions of ideal morality, but Christian ethics is fully identical with the ideal of rational morality." The Christian contribution "consists only in providing assistance in achieving this ideal, by the power of redemption which in the Christian community becomes available to the individual through his relationship to the person of Jesus."[17] For Troeltsch, Herrmann's ethic illustrates the fact that on the basis of Kant's practical philosophy, religion retains no independent meaning. Indeed, Christianity can at best serve only as a summarizing "of this morality which is both a conceptual necessity and yet at the same time subjective,"[18] as is the case in the thought of Kant himself or in Rationalism. Or, on the other hand, it serves "to promote moral behavior in general through providing assurance of the existence and reality of the divine power of the good and a readiness to provide for the forgiveness of sins."[19] By this last formulation, Herrmann carried forward the supernaturalistic form of his borrowing from Kant, in a manner similar to that of the nineteenth century renewal of theology, the movement in which Herrmann's own roots are to be found. Troeltsch was quite right in pointing out that on this line of argument Christian morality "had no new contribution to make in the determining of ethical goals, . . . and its higher powers are not the result of higher goals, but it might be said that it incarnates rational ethical goals in an absolutely complete form and provides the powers necessary to attain them."[20]

According to Troeltsch, religion and Christianity can exercise independent influence on modern ethical issues only when they expand Kant's basis of ethics in reason beyond the subjective limits he placed on it, so that its central task becomes the determination of the "objective values and goals of actions," as was the case with Schleiermacher and Hegel. "Thus ethics becomes cultural philosophy from an ethical point of view, in that it endeavors to demonstrate the necessity, reasonableness, and unity of the great, objective social goals which elevate the individual to a position of distinctive worth. In this way the goals of the state, society, art, science, the family, religion are made manifest, goals that as objective examples of the good determine human actions."[21] Troeltsch builds explicitly on Schleiermacher's concept of ethics—this "ethical high point of German idealism"[22]—and takes its completion as his goal. It is precisely in his theological ethics that Schleiermacher, according to Troeltsch, "did not begin" to draw the consequences of his "total picture."

To what extent is this the case? Troeltsch was thoroughly

aware that Christian ethics as the presentation of "the way the
Spirit of Christ works through the organism of his church" is
parallel to the general program of Schleiermacher's ethics as
the description of the way "reason acts on nature."[23] He was also
aware of the connection which the concept of the church
establishes between philosophical and theological ethics; it is
based on the former and forms the starting point of the latter.[24]
How was it then that he could hold that Schleiermacher's
theological ethics were not related to the major development of
his philosophical ethics? Troeltsch noted, first, that there was
no explicit treatment of the tensions between the way the
exponents of Christian piety presented the church in ethical
terms and the general institutions of secular society and its
culture. In Schleiermacher there was "no awareness of the
tension between action based on specifically Christian and
religious principles and that based on secular goals." It is a
question of issues which, if not caused by the secularization of
modern society, were intensified by it, and which Troeltsch (a
point to which we must return) regarded as the greatest
difficulty confronting a theological ethic.

But his criticism of Schleiermacher did not stop with the
observation that Schleiermacher did not give an adequate
description of the relationship of Christian ethics to the issues of
society and culture that lie outside of its domain. This point of
view only prepared the way for the fundamental objection—
that Schleiermacher did not derive from Christianity any
specifically Christian definition of the highest ethical goal, but,
by means of the concept of redemption, merely reinforced and
rounded out the basic direction of the moral spirit which had
been derived from another source. "The dominant concern is
no longer the problem of the essence of a specifically Christian
choice of ethical goals or the relationship of such a choice to
other goals, but the problem of how the moral spirit can attain
its full power and purity by the redemption through Christ and
in the church as the community of redemption."[25] This is
Troeltsch's description of the function which Christianity has in

Schleiermacher's thought for the universal ethical task, by conscious analogy to the content of the problem as determined earlier by Kant and Fichte. But he felt that by starting the ethical discussion with the concept of the highest good, Christianity would be able to make a more independent and significant contribution to establishing a basis for ethics.

Troeltsch held that this contribution is based on the heart of the message of Jesus. It is the "basic thought of Jesus' preaching," "the proclamation of the great, decisive moment, the coming of the Kingdom of God as the epitome of the complete rule of God, where God's will is done on earth as it is in heaven."[26] In Troeltsch's debate with Herrmann, this is where the key point in his argument is to be found: The gospel is not restricted to the concept of moral autonomy in the sense which that has in the ethics which Herrmann took over from Kant. "Quite to the contrary, Jesus announces clearly and with overruling emphasis a concrete goal and good, which produces through his affirmation actions which arise freely from the conscience, and at the same time hold up to the conscience a quite specific objective good and goal," that is, the Kingdom of God.[27] Only in terms of this basic thought is it possible to understand the "absolute subordination of the individual to society," which is expressed in the Christian concept of love, and which in Herrmann can assert itself only by a distortion of his ethical starting point, oriented as it is to Kant's thought. Troeltsch rightly asks whether it would be possible to imagine subordinating the individual to the "common good" unless "ethical demands were based on the thought of an all-inclusive divine purpose, in which the smallness of the individual is caught up in a great, eternal meaning of life derived from fellowship with God."[28] But then the concept of redemption can no longer be "the specific Christian element that is added on to the universal idea of a natural morality. . . . It must take second place. It cannot be fully independent, but must be seen as derived from the basic and primary idea, the idea of God and of an objective religious goal."[29]

This is an impressive demonstration of the greater ability to clarify as well as the theological superiority of the position that orients ethics to the question of the highest good, in contrast to Herrmann's approach. Its greater ability to clarify the New Testament data is seen in that Troeltsch was able to establish the basic significance of the coming Kingdom of God in the message of Jesus in its systematic relevance for ethics. He was the only systematic theologian of his time to do this, expressing it in terms of the eschatological future of the Kingdom of God, and of its consequent priority in time over all human actions.[30] From this starting point Troeltsch came to a more profound concept of redemption than Herrmann had, and one closer to the New Testament. For Herrmann the concept had a central function, but only in the subjectively limited sense of the nineteenth-century "renewal of theology," the tradition in which Herrmann stood.[31] On this point Troeltsch said: "It is a misunderstanding of Jesus' thought to hold that redemption frees us only from sin and moral weakness. It is rather the great redemption from grief over our finitude; it is the solution of the riddle of existence, and therefore something future. This future redemption is in contrast to present redemption only as the coming Kingdom of God is to the present kingdom, that is, as a mood of hope and confidence, as the heightened power of those who are permitted to see the goal that lies before them, those with whom the Bridegroom is present, who are able to see that for which those of old time longed."[32] In the later editions of his *Ethik,* Herrmann reacted to all this only in a critical comment on the basic nature of the ethics of concrete good which Troeltsch was advocating. He stated that the idea of the highest good is not able to provide a basis for the desired "unity of the will," because it is "not a concept clearly defined as to content," but one that "varies with the changing conditions of human life."[33] Herrmann thus had correctly perceived that the idea of the highest good had "its place" not in ethics, but in religion, "as the expression of the fulfillment of life for which we hope."[34] But this insight did not lead him to discover here, in analogy to the causal relationship of the Kingdom of God and the moral message of Jesus, the relationship between ethics and religion that he was seeking elsewhere, namely, in the context of the experience of guilt and the forgiveness of sin. This theological position of the "renewal theology" prevented him from discovering, as Troeltsch had, the insight into the systematic importance of the basic New Testament data. Perhaps too his prejudgment that the question of the highest Good as the starting point of ethics was consistently eudaemonistic, contributed to this result, although Plato's *Gorgias* had taught the priority of the good over the question of the pleasure to be derived from it.

Troeltsch's criticism of Herrmann's combining a concept of redemption that was isolated from that of the Kingdom of God and the idea of universal natural morality was also implicitly directed against Schleiermacher's Christian ethics, which had given a similar definition of the relationship of redemption to universal morality.[35] This was the case even though Schleiermacher differed from Kant in considering morality as still developing. Moreover, as Troeltsch points out, Herrmann accepted Schleiermacher's "basing Christian morality on a general law of morality incarnated in amazing manner in Jesus and on the redemptive imparting of the power to fulfill this law," but not without modifying "his corresponding ethicizing concept of religion."[36] Thus Troeltsch found in Herrmann's thought the Kantian basis of ethics combined with that idea of Schleiermacher's whose appearance in Christian morality he had criticized as Schleiermacher's deviation from the "great total picture" of his philosophical ethics, which was oriented to objective goals of conduct or concrete good. But is it not possible that this peculiarity of Schleiermacher's *Die christliche Sitte* is an indication that his concept of an ethic of the good and his concept of the highest good had already been developed along basic lines in a manner different from the development in Troeltsch's case?

In his ethics Schleiermacher derived his concept of the

highest good from his analysis of the action of reason on nature.[37]
The "unity of reason and nature" that is brought about by the
action of reason is also assumed to be the power working within
reason (§§80ff.) and under various aspects confronts us as a
"multiplicity of examples of the good." Thus "every unity of
specific aspects of reason and nature is a good" (§110). Just as
the concept of the good represents the object of action which is
to be produced by the action of reason but which is also at work
within it,[38] so is the concept of virtue the power that brings
about its realization (§111) and that of duty the combining of the
various activities with the universal good (§112). Therefore
although Schleiermacher accords to the concept of the good
(and above all to that of the highest good, as the epitome of all
good, §113), the precedence for the description of ethics,[39] this
concept is not presented as the goal of action, but designates the
unity of the action with its result. For Schleiermacher there is
no concept of the highest good that is prior to the moral process.
This finds expression also in Schleiermacher's position that
there is "no special knowledge" of the highest good, but only a
knowledge that is implicit in the "knowledge of the interrelat-
edness of all individual examples of good." Even the "Kingdom
of Heaven" as a designation for the completion of the individual
symbolic actions of religion is not in itself alone the epitome of
the highest good, but is so only in connection with the
completion of all other forms of activity.[40]

Thus for Schleiermacher the highest good is not prior to
action, but it is the product of moral actions and at the same
time is already at work in the power that produces this product
and in the development of its result. Thus in *Die christliche
Sitte* Schleiermacher is able to say that for the Christian
"redemption through Christ himself is the highest good, even if
in human history this is only represented by the Kingdom of
God; thus the Kingdom of God is the highest good, or for the
individual a place in that Kingdom, 'the inheritance in the
Kingdom of God.' "[41] Thus the Kingdom of God is not primarily
in the future, but is unfolding in Christian actions. This is seen

most clearly in Schleiermacher's statements about the "founding" of the Kingdom by Christ: "He has founded the Kingdom of God, toward which all Christian actions move, and he has indicated its basic features, so that all actions in the Christian church are nothing but the filling out of these basic features."[42] As a result he can also say that the Kingdom of God on earth is "nothing but the way in which one lives as a Christian, which is always to be made manifest through one's actions."[43] Thus the Kingdom of God is already a reality in the church, although still in the process of formation.

Troeltsch spoke differently of the Kingdom of God. For him it was—in agreement with the newer interpretation of Jesus' eschatological message by Johannes Weiss—essentially in the future, so that even Jesus distinguished between the future Kingdom of God and his own person. That was Troeltsch's decisive argument for the Christian legitimacy of his polemic against the claims for the absoluteness of Christianity as well as for every other historical manifestation. "Whatever role messianism may have played in the proclamation, in the total picture the person takes second place to the matter, the Kingdom of God. Here the Kingdom is that which is absolute, and it shows itself as such through its appeal to the purest and most inward needs of the soul, as well as in the certainty that it will soon miraculously be instituted by the Father, whose purpose for the world is thereby fulfilled."[44] For Troeltsch this future is both the end of history and something that lies beyond it, for "it is insane to want to have the absolute within history in an absolute manner at an individual point." Therefore "the living piety that is dependent on God holds the absolute truth of the future in reserve for the end of history."[45] In support of this position Troeltsch appeals to the proclamation of Jesus himself, because "it is precisely he who held absolute religion in reserve for what lies beyond history."[46] God is present to the pious only in "the revelations of the absolute that point to the future,"[47] and this future will be brought in only by God himself. The Kingdom of God is "not a human entity composed of those who acknowledge the law of autonomy as a law that God has placed in the human heart; it is a miraculous gift of God, something completely objective. It is the human community in total peace and total love, because it exists in total commitment and submission to the fully revealed Lordship of God. And because it stands under the special guidance and protection of God, it is a kingdom in which we see God and in which the merciful receive mercy. Troeltsch expressly adds that "it is exclusively a great act of God's mercy which brings about this ideal state, and the incredible concentration of all thought on this goal is revealed in that this act of grace is at our very door and the gospel is simply the exhortation to prepare for this act of grace."[48]

Giving the future of God's kingdom priority over all human actions is consistent with Troeltsch's concept of the highest good, which thereby takes on a decisively different nature from that of Schleiermacher. The clues to understanding what Troeltsch means when he speaks of purposes, goals, examples of the good that take form in history—especially in relation to the history of religion—are contained in his early writings. In his essay "The Christian World View and the Scientific Countercurrents,"[49] Troeltsch emphasized "the discovery of the meaning of ends for morality" in modern thought. "Without such an understanding of the concept of goals, the moral imperative would be senseless, incomprehensible, and a matter of indifference which would never be able to influence the will."[50] Here Troeltsch was emphasizing that spiritual goals are autonomous and underived. Two years later this approach was developed further in the religious-psychological positions of his essay on "The Independence of Religion." Here Troeltsch was concerned to present the independence of moral and aesthetic perceptions over against empirical experience. This did not involve "something generated by the activity of the spirit itself," but "the experience and perception of laws that are not empirical, that are independent of humans, and that are valid not for the individual, but for spirit in general, ideas which arise out of the depths of life."[51] Religious experience, however, is specifically different from such experiences of an ideal order, although the two belong close together. According to Troeltsch the difference lies "in the relationship found in the submission of religion to an infinite power (or at least infinite according to the standards of our understanding) in which the practical character of religion as striving for a highest good is ineradicable."[52] Here then the concept of the highest good is explicitly connected with the religious experience of a divine power that confronts our consciousness.[53] But Troeltsch held that it is not only ethical but also aesthetic experience which presupposes religious faith for the independence of its intellectual content. By this he meant that faith in such ordinances demands religious faith "as its basis" (ibid.). The manner in which this is the case is hinted at in a comment about the "self-evident authority" of ideal perceptions. Troeltsch says of them that they rest "on the power to arouse and lead the mind, a power to which we must surrender if we do not wish the seeds of these ideas to dry up."[54] It is not without reason that there appears here the concept of power, which four pages later designates the special object of religious experience.

By interpreting the good, or concrete examples of good, as goals, Troeltsch gave to their content a priority and autonomy in reference to moral actions that had no place in Schleier-macher's ethical concept, because he sought to bring the concept of the good into play in opposition to Kant's isolation of actions from their results. The distinct nature of Troeltsch's interest finds expression particularly in his concern with the autonomy of religion, not so much in relation to morality and metaphysics as in relation to empirical experience. The autonomy of religion, by virtue of the divine "power" that is manifest in it, forms the basis of the autonomy of other forms of intellectual perception in ethics and aesthetics. This indicates a quite different direction of thought from that found in Schleiermacher, but Troeltsch was not aware of this profound difference. He saw significant differences from Schleiermacher only in his concern to understand both religious experience in general and the course of the history of religions as the product of divine activity on humanity. In other respects his position was "that of Schleiermacher and the theologians and philosophers close to him."[55] Actually Schleiermacher was not unaware of the idea of divine activity on humanity in the history of religions. However, he did not see in it, as did Troeltsch, influences of a divine "power" that confronted humanity, because he did not regard religious experience as such to be an encounter of divine and human reality, but the arising of the transcendental ground of all being in the immediate human consciousness. Troeltsch's lack of clarity about the extent of this difference between Schleiermacher's thought and his own starting point adversely influenced the full development of his thought, especially in ethics.

Troeltsch felt that he was in agreement with Schleiermacher's assumption "that the human spirit is a coherent whole consisting of various developments of its basic drives that, impelled forward in a reciprocal relationship with the material world, create and complete the content of the spirit."[56] Troeltsch's most impressive description of how this occurs is found in his book "The Absoluteness of Christianity." "Alongside the system of natural requirements there arise in the depths of the soul ideals and meanings for life that are not mere products of history but are creative regulators of historical life, and that base their claims to validity not on the causal necessity that produced them but on their truth."[57] The starting point of this idea does remind us of Schleiermacher, as it does of Dilthey,[58] but with the emergence of ideals or values which are to be evaluated in terms of their claim to truth, something new has entered Troeltsch's thought, something that is distinctively his own contribution. In terms of the presupposition that all humans originally share the same spirit, we can understand how it is that—again in dependence on Schleiermacher—"the different values of mankind have something in common that by its very nature forces us to weigh values against each other and, out of the conviction which we attain in this way, to provide norms for and to evaluate both the individual and human history."[59] An additional consequence is "that in these individual formations there appear values of the same basic orientation which can be compared with and evaluated against each other. In this process a final decision is reached based on their inner truth and necessity."[60] Such a decision demands a standard, but this standard for forming judgments on these mutually conflicting ideals develops out of the conflict itself. The fact of this conflict reveals in itself a convergence toward a oneness of truth, a "common goal" of the "total process." "The standard can emerge only out of the free competition of these ideas with each other."[61] The absolute value which provides the definitive resolution to the struggle of ideas lies, to be sure, "beyond history, a realm accessible only to surmise and to faith."[62] But this goal which transcends history can "reveal" itself as an "always new creative synthesis, which gives to the absolute the form which is possible at that moment, and which yet brings with it the feeling that it is merely an approximation to the true, ultimate, and universal values."[63] Here too we are dealing "in every instance with goals and ideals that float before us and find specific expression in each form of life, though fully realized in none, and that as the ultimate goal of life lead us forward toward their fulfillment."[64]

In these thoughts Troeltsch developed an "ontology of human reason or . . . of the human spirit," which he felt rests on a belief "in the unity and upward aspiration of the spirit."[65] In the first point, the assumption of an original unity of spirit, his line of reasoning is closely related to Schleiermacher's thought, but it parts company with him in the idea of striving toward a goal. This is clear when he speaks of goals and ideals that "float before" our actions and especially when he speaks of the one ultimate goal that leads us on. Because his relationship to Schleiermacher is not clear, there is a certain ambiguity in Troeltsch's thought. It lies in the fact that on the one hand the total process of the formation and mutual interaction of the ideals can be described as the working out of the original unity of the spirit,[66] but on the other hand, and decisively so in Troeltsch, this unity itself can be understood as something future, so that in the convergence of the cultivation of the mind the power of its common future destiny finds expression. That which is common and universally valid in historical systems is, as Troeltsch explicitly stated, not to be grasped by means of a general concept abstracted from them. In fact, it is "not the concept of an actual general truth that is fully expressed in its human realization, but the concept of something that floats before us all, for which the way is prepared in history with varying strength and clarity, but which still floats before us."[67] "As something complete and whole it remains beyond history," as the future of the absolute, which lies beyond history.[68]

By such formulations the intellectual unity of individual forms of ideals and goals is postponed into the future. The convergence of historical systems within the historical process and the unity and commonality contained therein are understood as the expression of their future destiny. Troeltsch, however, spoke in other places of this commonality as the result of an original unity of spirit, an assumption that shows the influence of Schleiermacher's philosophy of identity and of Kantian *a priori* assumptions. The tension in Troeltsch's thought between the two poles of origin and the future remained unresolved to the end. In one of his last lectures he said: "And just as a final common goal lies in the unknown future, perhaps in the world beyond, so there is a common ground in the divine spirit which moves irresistibly into the light and into our consciousness. It is included in the final end, and it is out of its final unity with finite spirit that the whole manifold movement emerges."[69] Troeltsch speaks explicitly here of two "poles," the "divine ground and the divine goal." In his theological writings the point of view of the goal dominates, but Troeltsch never definitively accorded it precedence over the concept of the absolute origin, or incorporated it into the idea of the future of the absolute, because he always shied away from providing a more precise explanation of his concept of the absolute.

Inasmuch as Troeltsch's theological metaphysics made the contrast between the absolute as the future of history and all historical, relative representations of it, he was able to give clear expression to the eschatological meaning of Jesus' message about the Kingdom of God. It was along this line that he developed, in his essay on "Basic Problems of Ethics," the idea of "the dominance of eschatology in the gospel as the magnificent expression of the unique value of the religious goal." All this-worldly considerations and goals "are stripped of their importance and outmoded" under the influence of the nearness of the eschatological expectation of the end."[70] Troeltsch not only did an impressive job of working out the inner logic of this exegetical material, but he also knew how to combine it with later developments in Christian ethics, in spite of the difference in content. In doing so he did not find it necessary to condemn the later openness to the world as a falling away from the gospel, or to water down the radicalism of early Christian eschatology through hermeneutical stratagems. He simply rejected Renan's position that because of its radically eschatological nature the early Christian ethic was to be "regarded as the original form of monastic life."[71] Christianity's concept of a personal God contained from the first "the thought of a purpose that molded and sanctified the world" and placed on "human undertakings the necessity of sanctifying the goals of the world and placing them in the service of its total goal by means of a community of persons." In order that this tendency which is founded on the Christian idea of God might exert its influence, it is "only necessary that the religious goal lose the force of its immediate fulfillment, which would sublimate everything else. Only under this condition can it be recognized as the highest goal which governs all else, and it can emerge only out of eschatology. But it can continue to exert influence even when its immediate realization is postponed into the future, and it can find new life only by being immersed in the picture of the classic primordial time, when it alone confronted the human heart with the power of present reality. The world and its ordinances were not then rejected, but they were adopted for the rest of time as something that came from God, even though they did not have any worth in and of themselves. Now they were once more to come to light permanently and thereby confront us with the positive tasks of sanctifying and overcoming them. For the sake of God who is the God of creation, and from whom the world and all its concrete good stems, as soon as the world becomes a continuous field for work it is to be evaluated positively, and its goals are to be merged, insofar as possible, with the final goal which God has revealed."[72] By this Troeltsch was giving an answer to the difficult question of the continuing significance of the early Christian expectation of the end, and to the question of the theological overcoming and interpretation of the fact that this hope had faded so soon. These are answers that are as superior to the theses of catastrophe in the so-called "consistent eschatology" of the school of Albert Schweitzer as they are to the theories of a decline of Christian history from its early heights, theories that were based on the observation of the great distance of post-apostolic and contemporary Christianity from their origins.

This thesis of Troeltsch's, which even today has lost none of its central validity,[73] may be regarded as one of his most significant contributions to theology. If from the outset it had received the acceptance that it deserves, the theology of this century could have avoided many detours and many of the unnecessary qualms of conscience that it has felt with respect to the course of the history of Christianity. It could also have avoided the tormenting problems and hermeneutical contortions that have resulted from an unhistorical concept of the authority of Scripture that grew out of the urge to establish a direct connection between the early Christian statements of faith and the present day. The abiding significance of the early Christian view of the primacy of the coming Lordship of God as the highest good beyond all other expressions of the good led Troeltsch to the problem of the "tension" that arises between the highest good of God's sovereignty and the concrete moral good of culture, derived from life in the world and independent of Christianity in its setting of goals, its development, and the nature of its goals as self-directed in their own sphere."[74] Troeltsch regarded this not as a problem that first arose in the modern, secular world, in relation to its Christian origins, but as a fundamental problem that had accompanied Christianity from its beginnings and that grew out of a situation more common and widespread, that of the polarity between the "two principal types of goals, the religious and those related only to this world." This is the basis of the "richness of our life," and also of its difficulty. "It is the source from which again and again there arises the passionate struggle to achieve unity." The fundamental situation according to Troeltsch is that "morality by its nature is not something unified, but is fragmented, and that man progresses within a multiplicity of moral goals, the unification of which is the problem and not the starting point." But it is because of this, according to Troeltsch, that moral life must take religion into account. "The unification must always be developed in terms of the religious-moral concept."[75]

The general polarity between religious goals and secular cultural goals will, Troeltsch felt, of necessity become a problem within Christianity. Nevertheless, because religion proceeds "from the creative, all-encompassing will of God, establishing religious goals cannot simply mean providing replacements for this-worldly goals." "The Christian belief in God, with its positive evaluation of the world that God created, must make it possible to include this-worldly goals within the absolute goal of community with God."[76] Troeltsch therefore regarded it as an ethical task in each new situation to find a compromise[77] between this-worldly goals that are "in the service of the state, law, science, and art" and the demands of the religious goal, whose power consists in that it is indispensable for the unification of the worldly goals.

This point of view is basic to Troeltsch's great work on the social teachings of the Christian churches and groups. Developments in the early church led to an increasingly positive evaluation of secular relationships in such questions as property, labor, the permanent structure of society, trade, family, slavery, and state. This appeared to him as an expression of a "compromise" with the world, not least in reference to the formulation of the theory of a creative natural law related to the conditions that resulted from the Fall.[78] The Christian Middle Ages developed the ideal of a unified Christian culture, but in fact this ideal rested on earlier compromises with the world, and, according to Troeltsch, led to counter movements of "sectarian" renewal of the early Christian ideals. These counter movements, he felt, proved to be decisive factors in the collapse of unified medieval culture.[79] He also held that modern Christianity had not attained the comparable stabilization of such a compromise, though it came close to it in Neo-Calvinism, the influence of which, however, he regarded as on the wane. The task still confronts us.[80]

However plausible this concept seems at first sight, its theoretical bases suffer from the lack of clarity which has been noted again and again in this essay. An initial indication of this is the lack of congruence between the systematic concept of a compromise of religious and secular ends and goals, on the one hand, and the insight provided by Troeltsch's explanation of the continuity of the historical development of Christianity from the eschatological radicalism of its beginnings to the positive acceptance of the world and its conditions in the following age. If this development is grounded in the Christian idea of God itself, insofar as God is the creator of this world and desires its well-being, then it does not seem necessarily to be a compromise if Christianity opens itself to the conditions of the cultural world in which its message is proclaimed, in order to integrate them into itself. It is the way in which such integration is accomplished that is decisive for the question of whether or not it has been achieved at the price of a compromise with conditions and views that are in opposition to the Christian faith. Such a compromise, however, can of course not be termed an ethical task, but it indicates the failure to perform that task, the failure of the duty to accomplish a Christian "transformation" of those things which are the givens of society.[81] Troeltsch used the term "compromise" in a wider sense for every encounter of Christianity with the actual conditions of the world of culture. Still, if that is mandated by the concept of God itself, then the concept of "compromise" is misleading. It presents too superficial a description of the "cultural synthesis" that has been achieved again and again in the history of Christianity, the credibility of which depends on the conviction of its Christian authenticity.

Troeltsch's concept of a compromise betrays a conception of the Kingdom of God in terms of a contrast between the absolute and the relative. It is here that we see the one-sided nature of his interpretation of the Kingdom of God as the absolute future which as such is in contrast to the world of history. In Troeltsch's writings the confrontation between this world and the future world of the absolute in the eschatological message of early Christianity is forcefully expressed, but that is not true in the same way of the presence of this future in the coming of Jesus and in his person.[82] The problem can be traced back to Troeltsch's basic concept of "goal." The category of goal unites present and future only by keeping them separate from each other.[83] When the future that has been our goal becomes present, it ceases to be a goal. And when the Kingdom of God as the highest goal is only contrasted to the present, the paradoxical result is that a this-worldly sphere is made autonomous, and in it the dependence of human behavior on the future is made concrete in a multiplicity of this-worldly goals. But this reveals the same unfulfilled nature of the present world, the "inadequacy of worldly goals," for the sake of which the thought of a final, unified, all-encompassing "goal" has been put forward again and again.[84] If, however, worldly goals, which are inevitably insufficient, are by their nature unable to achieve independent status, how is it possible to speak seriously of their independence and autonomy?[85] It seems rather to be the case that these worldly goals, insofar as they are made autonomous, are brought by human experience to the point which Troeltsch repeatedly termed the situation in which Christianity began: "Christian morality could arise only in a situation in which worldly goals no longer gave satisfaction, in the disordered life of a people, and it found the soil out of which it actually developed in the world of ancient culture, which had found on its own that worldly goals cannot prove satisfying."[86] It is possible to find a confirmation of this insight of Troeltsch's in the fact that the experience of the shattering of the world of European Christian culture in the First World War led, at least in theology, to a new acceptance of the "omnipotence of total control which the eschatological concept exercised over the gospel," a new "subjugation of all thoughts to the immediate sovereignty of the final goal."[87] Barth's attempt to use the concept of the sovereignty of God as a new basis for theology had its roots, if not its motivation, in Troeltsch's interpretation of Jesus' proclamation of the Kingdom of God, and this was also its problematical legitimation. In his carrying out of this approach Barth was unable to overcome the basic problem of Troeltsch's theology as it involves the category of goal—the dualism of Kingdom of God and world. To be sure, it is not so much that he made this dualism into a problem as that he employed it under the assumption of that "absolute distinction between Christianity and the non-Christian world," an assumption which Troeltsch saw Herrmann as endeavoring to demonstrate.[88] Barth accepted this distinction as given, not only in reference to non-Christian religion, but—going beyond Herrmann—also in reference to all "natural" experience. It was the exclusive nature of his theology of revelation that thwarted Barth's intention to think of the world without any qualifications as God's world, and that led instead to a self-imposed isolation of Christian faith and thought in an imaginary realm apart from the real human world. Troeltsch saw the dangers of

Herrmann's dualism, but he shared the problems inherent in this position, although they took on a different form in his thought. For Troeltsch the dualism between present and absolute future in his category of goal led to his making the worldly present state of the intellect autonomous in its relation to the absolute, in spite of the recognition that all historical manifestations are relative. But this autonomy was again negated by the question of "power" that forms the basis of the autonomy of intellectual "ideals." In any case, by the concept of goal Troeltsch brought the world of human experience and cultural activity into relationship to the highest good of the Kingdom of God. To think of the Kingdom of God as the highest good demands more than the concept of goal can provide. In any case it must be thought of as the highest good *for humankind,* and therefore not as a contrast to human experience and the human world, but in relationship with it, and as something that includes life and the world. In this way the Kingdom of God must show that it is the highest human good, and only insofar as this happens is the inclusion of ethics in dogmatics accomplished, a task to which Barth saw himself called by Troeltsch. This must be done if the priority of the Kingdom of God is to be taken seriously in theological thought.[89]

6

LUTHER'S DOCTRINE
OF THE TWO KINGDOMS

I

In various statements during the last war, Karl Barth asserted that Luther's theology and Lutheranism share the responsibility for making National Socialism possible. He held that the Lutheran doctrine of the independent "authority of the state" "provided a certain amount of breathing space for German paganism" in that it "separated the created world and law from the gospel."[1] This made it possible for the Nazi movement to "disguise itself as the establishment of true ruling authority" (p. 121). According to Barth, "Martin Luther's error in respect to the relationship of law and gospel, of secular and spiritual order and power" (p. 113) was to be found in his making the secular realm independent and thereby immunizing it against the comprehensive claim of the Lordship of Christ over all realms of life.

Is this critique appropriate to Luther's doctrine of the two kingdoms, the Kingdom of God and the kingdom of the world, and of the two ways God rules (his "regiments") over these two kingdoms? There has been much disagreement on this point. It has repeatedly been pointed out that Luther was by no means speaking of the complete independence of the state from the gospel, nor did he advocate a subjection and obedience that would renounce all right to criticize the ruler. Also he made the state subordinate to the Lordship of God, the same God who

112

ruled in the church through the Holy Spirit. Furthermore Luther ascribed to the preaching office of the church a responsibility even toward the ruling power. Part of the task of the preaching office was that the preacher should "inform and instruct all social classes how they should conduct themselves in their offices and ranks, so that they would act justly for God. . . . For a preacher confirms, strengthens, and helps uphold all authority, all temporal peace, rebukes the disorderly, teaches obedience, morality, discipline, and honor, teaches the office of father, mother, children, servants, in sum, all worldly offices and ranks."[2] That the confirming and strengthening of authority was not to be expressed in a fawning servility, but under certain circumstances in severe criticism, Luther himself demonstrated with the unyielding courage of his convictions on numerous occasions, including the Peasant Wars. He found the basis for such criticism in the "natural law" which he contrasted to the positive law established by human authority, and to which he affirmed that the state was subject.[3] Luther's emphasis on the independence of the state thus was by no means carte blanche for the ruler to act arbitrarily, even though the natural law to which the authorities were subject was not understood in the sense of an eternal law, but in the elastic sense of "natural law, which is permeated by reason" (p. 279). Thus Luther also demanded that "reason should remain the supreme law and the master of all law" (p. 272). He held that reason dealt with laws and ordinances in the spirit of fairness and that it altered them in accordance with circumstances.[4]

Luther held that certain truths belong together: that the one God is Lord not only in the church but also in secular government, that rulers are bound by that which reason recognizes as natural and just, and that the preaching of the church also has the responsibility of instructing secular authorities and strengthening them through criticism and exhortation. The intimate relationship of these themes to each other is seen in striking manner in Luther's teaching that the voice of reason and nature is identical with that of love. "For nature teaches, as does love, that I do unto others as I would have them do unto me." Therefore Luther can contrast the "law of love and nature" to the books of the jurists, and say that the latter are to be evaluated in terms of the former (p. 279).

All this shows that Luther did not intend to abandon the state to the caprice of those in power, or to allow it to go its own way, independent of the will of God. This does not, however, exclude the possibility that in Luther's distinction between two realms and two "regiments" there might be factors that, taken alone, would move in another direction, as can be seen in the themes mentioned above, and would tend to separate secular authority from the context of those principles that motivate Christianity. One such feature is the fact that Luther gave singularly formal expression to the basic concepts that define the state, that is, the secular authority, when he said that it "possesses the secular sword and law in order to punish the evil and protect the pious" (p. 248). This expression is formal especially because it ignores the concrete historical ground on which any political life in community takes its specific form. In particular, Luther, with the general nature of his concept of secular authority, is not concerned with whether or not it involves a political life in community in a country of Christendom *(christianitas)*. Luther could even emphasize that the heathen "in such matters are much more clever than Christians,"[5] and point to the Ottoman state as an example of secular authority that was worthy of emulation. Such statements imply a concept of political authority that is neutral over against all specifically Christian motivation. It might be asked whether natural law and reason can still have the same concrete meaning under such different circumstances, and especially whether they can be identical with "the law of love" in both instances.

The problems that arise here will be looked at later in this essay. At this point it is necessary to keep only one thing in mind: It is not in the complex total picture of Luther's statements on political ethics, but rather in his line of thought found in the formal definition of concepts which he intends to be basic, that he tends to regard the principles on which the state rests as a matter of indifference in their relation to the religious ground on which concrete political life in community is established. This tendency seems, as will become even clearer, to be in tension with other thoughts of Luther, some of which have already been touched on briefly here and which stress the unity of the Christian God as the one who rules alone through both the spiritual and the secular power, so that the Christian office of preaching has the important task of instructing the secular ruler concerning his duties. But because of the neutrality of the formally expressed concept of secular authority and its responsibilities toward the concrete unity which political life in community has with the specific religion of the region over which it rules, it is extremely difficult to reject out of hand the objections which Barth has raised against the doctrine of the two realms. Even though they do not apply to the whole of Luther's position, they are relevant to the not-insignificant line of thought expressed in his involved and complex statements about questions of political life.

The observation that in Luther's doctrine of the two realms there is a certain independence and arbitrariness of political authority involves two further problems, which must be mentioned at least briefly here. The first is Troeltsch's[6] accusation of a double standard in Luther's position that the Christian as Christian accepts injustice against himself, but as the bearer of a secular office he makes use of the means of force and of the sword. In this connection it has been pointed out that for Luther a Christian's assuming of a secular office is motivated by love, which, for the sake of our fellow humans, dedicates itself to the preservation of public peace, and that because of human sin this cannot be done without the use of force. As correct as this position is, there still remains some uneasiness over the fact that by taking over a public office the Christian becomes a member of an institution which only seldom can be influenced in any decisive way by his personal motivation.[7] The nature of institutions is not simply identical with the attitudes of the persons who represent them. But neither is it the case that this identity is contained in timeless general responsibilities; rather, it takes its characteristics from the specific historical conditions in which it functions. This again raises the question whether it is appropriate to regard the nature of a political order as independent of the historical ground of the religious and cultural tradition in which it has arisen.

Did Luther limit his statements on political life to the persons involved in it, or did he include the institutions in which the activities of these persons are carried out? In recent studies of Luther's doctrine of the two realms the dominant tendency has been to regard the Kingdom of God and the kingdom of the world not as realms in which authority is exercised, but as designations for two distinct groups of persons. Luther generally phrased this distinction as the contrast between two groups. "Here we must divide Adam's children and all humans into two parts, those who belong to the kingdom of God, and those who belong to the kingdom of the world."[8] To God's kingdom belong "all who truly believe in Christ and are under Christ; for Christ is the King and the Lord in the kingdom of God." To the kingdom of the world—and thus under the law—"belong all who are not Christians" (p. 251), and they are compelled by the secular government, which is ordained by God "to act in a peaceful and orderly manner without any thanks for doing so" (ibid.). Thus in reality the distinction of the two kingdoms and the consequent distinction of two ways in which God exercises his rule leads to the division of humans into two groups. This observation, however, must not, as has recently been pointed out,[9] lead to the opinion that Luther was not at all interested in the institutional form that human activities take. Indeed, Luther's ethics of vocation shows that he had clearly in mind that human activities were connected in a concrete manner with specific offices and callings. The concrete institutional nature of activities in this sense is even one of his central insights. Nonetheless, Luther seems to have regarded the differentiation of roles and "offices"—from the roles of father, mother, child, and servant to that of ruler—as something given. He scarcely seems to have been interested in the concrete system of roles in society in terms of their historical origins, their arbitrary nature, and their possibly being subject to change.

This leads us then from another angle back to Luther's basic problem of granting independent authority to the secular realms of life. The tendency of some of his basic statements to regard the religious nature of the ground of political life as a matter of indifference corresponds to his remarkably unreflective adoption of a given system of roles, involving the concrete behavior of individuals in the context of life in society. On the other hand, Luther took theologically motivated positions in respect to the institutional problems of his time, especially in the area of the politics of education. Thus we once again have the impression that the complex picture of Luther's position on political life is permeated by tensions which apparently found no systematic resolution. In order better to understand these tensions, we now turn to the historical roots of Luther's doctrine of the two kingdoms.

II

It has already been pointed out that Luther combines his distinction between two kingdoms or realms with the distinction between two ways in which God rules, two "regiments" of God. The first concept, the contrast of two realms, is derived from Augustine, while the second, that of two ways in which God rules, goes back to the medieval theory of two forces in Christendom, one secular and the other spiritual. Luther's original contribution to the theology of politics is his bringing together these two lines of thought.

For Luther the Kingdom of God, and for Augustine the *civitas Dei*, stood in contrast to the kingdom of the world (which for Augustine was the kingdom of the devil), as one human group to another. Both groups had their beginning with Adam, and we read in Luther that Adam's children, and that means all humans, are divided into two categories. The ones who are God's citizens are recognizable in that they love God even to the point of denying themselves. The others love themselves to the point that they hate God. Nietzsche's phrasing of the matter cannot be improved upon: "If there were a God, who could bear not to be God?" As for the second group, its characteristic expression of arrogance, *superbia*, is found, according to Augustine, in political life and political authority. This is especially true of the Roman Empire, the collapse of which came about in the West through Alaric's conquest of Rome in A.D. 410, the occasion for the writing of *De Civitate Dei*.[10]

In his contrasting of the two *civitates*, Augustine stood in the tradition of Jewish and Christian apocalyptic, which looked forward to the coming of the Kingdom of God in contrast to the succession of empires, in which human wickedness toward God was especially conspicuous. God's kingdom is of course a future kingdom, but the godly who at present are already hoping for the realization of God's rule will share in it, according to both Jewish and Christian conceptions, through the resurrection of the dead. The godly of Old Testament times, even back to the earliest human ancestors, will share in the coming Kingdom of God. Thus there arose the concept of two human groups, whose opposition to each other began in the days of Adam. In the New Testament this concept found expression, or a point of contact, in Paul, who drew the contrast between Christ, the new man, and the first Adam, representative of the old humanity that was doomed to die.[11]

In the perspective of apocalyptic, the political structure of the world empires usually appeared in a negative light. Augustine, however, in spite of his sharp criticism of the striving for political power and especially of Roman *superbia*, still maintained that the political order had a positive value insofar as it at least assured a provisional state of peace. Humans, because of their self-love, are not able to attain to the true fulfillment of the longing for peace that is innate in their nature, but it is still possible even under those circumstances to attain to an earthly copy of the heavenly peace, which God alone can provide. Christians, the citizens of the *civitas Dei*, are not to be indifferent to this earthly peace, but are to pursue it, preserve it, and support the institutions that promote it. Here Augustine expressed, in line with Paul's statements in Romans 13, the positive relationship of the Christian to political life, insofar as it involves the preservation of peace. He does not, as Luther later did, designate the positive function of political peace as the result of God's worldly rule, but the content of Luther's doctrine has its origin here. Luther too specified the task of secular authority as that of preserving and protecting the peace. He added to this the task of preserving justice,[12] and especially the concept of secular rule, in contrast to God's spiritual rule over his church.

The distinction between God's two methods of exercising rule, as has been pointed out, had its origin in the Middle Ages. In the unified Christian culture of the Middle Ages there was no concrete expression of a non-Christian society, a *civitas Diaboli*, standing in contrast to the Christian church and having its own realm. Thus emphasis came to be placed on the distinction between spiritual and secular power within Christendom. This distinction had a prior history in the contrast of bishop and emperor in the Byzantine Empire, where the emperor as a member of the church was subject to the office of the bishop, just as the bishop as citizen of the kingdom was a subject of the emperor. The contrast of bishop and emperor developed especially as the result of the relationship of Ambrose of Milan to the emperor Theodosius the Great. The formulation of principles that proved basic to the Middle Ages he found in a statement that Pope Gelasius I wrote of the emperor Anastasius during the Monophysite quarrels: "There are two, O noble emperor, by whom this world is principally ruled—the holy authority of the bishops and the royal authority. Of these two the priestly power is more weighty in that at the judgment it must give account to God for these kings who rule mankind."[13] The "world" which here is ruled by these powers, *auctoritas* and *potestas*, is coextensive with Christendom. It is not a matter of a world that differs from it or is even hostile to it. The preeminence of the priestly *auctoritas* as established by Gelasius is not to be understood as a claim to political precedence, but is to be taken in the sense of moral precedence. In this sense it was not accepted by the Byzantine Empire, when it was restored by Justinian I, but it was adopted by Charlemagne, or perhaps by his adviser Alcuin. Nevertheless, the emperors in the West as in the East understood themselves as the successors of Christ, that is, as earthly representatives of the heavenly royal power of Christ, while for them the pope was only the vicar of Peter.[14]

Thus the emperor himself was the holder of a spiritual office, which included responsibility for the well-being of Christendom on earth, and not only for that of secular rulers. The two powers—*auctoritas* and *regnum*—were not yet distinguished as spiritual and secular power, although the terminological distinction between *potestas spiritualis* and *potestas saecularis* was found in Alcuin.[15] The emperors understood their *regnum* in direct connection with the heavenly Jerusalem, which was symbolically represented in the imperial crown, as the earthly form of the Kingdom of God. On this basis the emperor Otto and his successors laid claim to rights in the church, as had the Byzantine emperors, especially the right to appoint bishops. Only after the conclusion of the struggle for this right in the investiture controversy was the emperor really restricted to the exercise of secular power alone, although the Hohenstaufen emperors, who regarded themselves as the continuation of the Roman Empire and thus appealed to the Roman laws of the Code of Justinian, still claimed to be the secular representatives of the unity of Christendom. These ideas continued to exert influence down to the time of Charles V and even beyond. They were not, however, any longer able to establish the independence of imperial power as a sacral office of Christendom. On the contrary, the conferring of imperial power *(translatio imperii)*, not only to the individual emperor at his coronation but also by Rome to the German empire of the Middle Ages, was claimed as a right of the church (that is, of the pope)—to the extent that Boniface VIII regarded the conferring of secular power in Christendom in general as the prerogative of the church, and therefore regarded not only the emperor but also the kings as feudal vassals of the church.

In addition to losing its independent sacral function, from the eleventh century on the office of emperor lost even its claim to universality. Although Rainald von Dassel still clung to the emperor's claim to authority over the kingdoms of western Europe, the kingdoms acknowledged the emperor only as first in rank but did not regard themselves as legally dependent on him,[16] and from the end of the twelfth century on the kings even asserted their equality with the emperor.[17] This change in the understanding of imperial power naturally did not occur to the same extent and at the same pace in the emperors' understanding of themselves. Nothing reveals the change more clearly than the fact that in the fourteenth century the leaders in the struggle for the independence of imperial power from the pope, that is, Marsilius of Padua and William of Ockham, sought to establish this independence only as pertaining to secular power, without reference to any special position of the imperial office in the body of Christendom. It seems that at that time, the independence of the emperor from the pope was conceivable only at the price of a total secularization and through restricting the church to spiritual concerns, in the sense of the Franciscan movement.

This brings us to a decisive point in the historical background of Luther's concept of secular power. Luther still regarded the emperor as sovereign over the princes, and consequently it was only with hesitation that he granted to the Protestant princes the right to armed resistance against the emperor, until he became convinced in 1530 that the power of the regional princes was a direct power and that the emperor held only a power derived through his election by the electors. Moreover,

Luther no longer regarded the office of emperor as a sacral office within Christendom. The transition represented earlier by Marsilius and Ockham to a purely secular conception of imperial power had become for Luther a self-evident basis for his statements. Even if we must regard this as a failure to recognize the problem, it would be anachronistic to blame Luther for it. In this matter he shared the point of view of his time, which must be seen in its relation to the situation of that age more clearly than is usually done in the discussions of Luther's doctrine of the two kingdoms, and which must not be too quickly interpreted from the perspective of the modern separation of state and church as being universally valid.

Luther's evaluation of the imperial office as a purely secular power is characteristic of his relationship to the medieval theory of the two powers. In terms of historical development, it is understandable that Luther (like Marsilius and Ockham before him), at least in his basic theoretical statements, no longer was thinking of a polarity between two powers in the framework of a united Christendom. His political thought was based on the presupposition that the independence of the secular power, with which Luther was primarily concerned over against the usurpations of the church, had to be based on the universally distinctive nature and autonomy of political authority as such. It was not based, however, on the independence of political functions in a society permeated by Christianity and in the context of the Christian tradition. In distinction to the Byzantine concept of the state, as well as to that of the medieval theory of two powers, Luther no longer regarded the question of a special structure of political life within Christendom as a problem. In fact, Luther's doctrine of the two realms is, as a Christian theological theory, an expression of Christian self-understanding, a modification of the Christian definition of the essence of political life in its relationship to the church. The relationship of religious and political authority is, in spite of the variety of the ways in which it has been expressed in the course of Christian history, a highly characteristic feature of the structure of society as brought about by Christendom, a feature that makes obvious the eschatological consciousness of Christendom, its knowledge of the provisional nature of all present social structures in the light of man's final destiny before God.

Luther's doctrine of the two kingdoms takes its place among the various expressions of this basic motif. Luther himself was aware of this insofar as he presented his ideas as a theological doctrine, but not in the sense that these ideas were also the expression of a history of human society decisively influenced by Christendom or that they then interacted with that history. Luther was prevented from recognizing this by his understanding of the authority of Scripture as a divinely sovereign counterpoint to all human history. Thus he did not consider what it might mean to investigate the task and significance of political power in the context of a Christendom that had developed, not only under the influence of the Word of God, but also in the arena of history. Instead he followed the tradition of Marsilius and Ockham in his theoretical reflections on the theme of political sovereignty, as if it were a matter of total indifference to him whether one were dealing with forms of political life that had developed in the context of Christianity, or those that had developed in a totally different manner. To be sure, in his doctrine he presents an interpretation and justification of political power in terms of Christian theology, but he does it in such a way that our self-understanding in this sense has no significance for the nature of secular power as such and is relevant only for those Christians who hold secular office. Luther, however, did not consistently hold to this basic theoretical viewpoint which had been abstracted from the data provided by a society that had been historically formed by Christendom, by *christianitas*. As Marsilius and Ockham had done, Luther too assigned to this abstract point of view a function within Christendom in the debates over the relationship between the church and political power. This involved the basis for the claim of the political powers to independence from the hierarchy of the church within the context of the society that existed within Christendom. Moreover, at other points in Luther's thought, it was the actually existing interrelationship of Christianity and society that was in the forefront, rather than the theoretical abstraction of his doctrine. Early in his career in his *Letter to the Christian Nobility* of 1520 he ascribed to those who held political power a responsibility for the well-being of the church within the life of Christendom. Later on, though not without hesitation, he acknowledged that those special members of the Christian community had responsibility to exercise oversight over the organization of the church. He recognized the meaning of religious unity for the unity of political life in community, and at the same time he took account of the right and duty of the preacher to instruct the rulers. Let us keep this last aspect in mind and attempt to imagine how different the social position of the church would appear in a state that really was alien and hostile to Christianity, and in which the church at best was tolerated only as a voluntary organization, but one that was politically loyal and thus without that right to open criticism which Luther assumed as a matter of course for Christian preaching. It then becomes clear how great the difference is between the historical setting of his own political theory and that society which was in fact characterized by the given framework of Christian tradition. In terms of the problems of Luther's era and in the light of his concern to justify the independence of the state within late medieval society over against the church's claims to supremacy, it is understandable that Luther did not take into account the historical setting of his doctrine when he formulated his basic statements about political power. Instead of this he presented in general terms an abstract secular power without considering any ways in which it might have been modified in the context of Christendom. This circumstance explains the tensions which we noted at the beginning of this essay in Luther's statements concerning secular power and its relationship to the church.

Let us now look at the systematic form which Luther's theological interpretation gave to the relationship between the church and autonomous political authority. First, Luther restricted the tasks of the church to the spiritual realm, to the inner life. In this he was not merely following an old tradition in philosophy and theology, that of the distinction between the inner and the outer man and the assigning of them to two groups of humans, the old Adam and the new. In developing these ideas he was much more following trends in the understanding of the church which were in line with contemporary Franciscan spirituality and numerous variations of thought in the late Middle Ages, and with the resulting reaction against the secularized state of the church.

Second, Luther went a step farther in that he regarded both the spiritual power and the secular as God's ways of exercising his rule, and not as powers entrusted to humans. By this change of emphasis from human sovereignty to God's direct activity (which was characteristic for and central to the whole of Luther's thought and central in his doctrine of justification), Luther had moved beyond the range of problems involved in the medieval theory of the two powers. It remains doubtful, however, that he was able to integrate the problems and viewpoints of that theory into his own system. But the interpretation of the two "regiments" as God's ways of ruling made it possible for him to give a theological interpretation to the purely secular basis of political authority; that is, he taught that God himself directly committed authority even to non-Christians, and he then was able to combine this view of the state with his own understanding of the church by considering them from the same point of view. In this way Luther could give expression to his view that while in relation to God man can only be a recipient, he still is called in both the secular and the spiritual offices to share in God's work of love in the world.

In the third place, Luther combined the distinction between two "regiments" with the Augustinian distinction between two realms or kingdoms. The function of this combination, and its achievement, was that first of all it established the necessity of political authority and at the same time set limits on its claims. The task of political authority in the kingdom of the world—that is, among those humans who have fallen victim to sin and the devil—is to seek to establish external peace and justice, to hold the effects of sin in check. It follows from this that political authority encounters its limit when it touches the inwardness of human life, and that it cannot dictate to the human conscience and to human convictions. On this basis and within these limits of secular authority a specific theological point of view found expression in Luther, one that could be effective historically only within a society shaped by Christianity. In Luther's thought the elements of this theological qualification on political authority consist only of the doctrine of sin and the distinction between the outer and the inner man. The relation to redemption remains extrinsic to the theoretical concept of secular authority. It is contained only in the relationship (which is external to the secular order) between God's will to preserve creation and God's intention to redeem mankind, realized in Christ and mediated through the church. This relationship is not a part of political life as such. It is useless to search in Luther's writings for a relationship of political life to the Christian hope, to the heavenly Jerusalem, in which human political destiny would be so fully realized that there would no longer be any need of a specific church or of any temple. Thus for him political order does not belong to human destiny as such, to that which will find its fulfillment in the future Kingdom of God. Instead, that order is only an emergency measure which God has provided against sin, a divine interim that will disappear in the eschatological future, and of which the Christian in himself has now no need.

III

On closer examination, Luther's doctrine of the two kingdoms and of God's two "regiments" is seen as an expression of political thought deeply colored by the thought of its own time in the context of the transmission of Christian theology. This raises the question of what its permanent significance may be. The results of this present discussion would hardly justify regarding Luther's doctrine as the final and decisive word for a Christian theory of politics. The synthesis of the Christian tradition of political theology which Luther's theory presents is too one-sided for that. Central motifs of this tradition are lacking, such as the positive relation of hope to the heavenly Jerusalem, to the coming kingdom of God, to political life. The interpretation of the state as merely God's emergency arrangement against sin remains too limited, though the partial truth it embodies cannot be denied. The lack of any positive relationship is closely connected to the fact that Luther did not take into account the question of specifically Christian features in the structure of political life, and therefore reflected only quite inadequately the historical basis on which his own theological treatment of the theory of secular power rested. His abstract concept of secular authority, divorced as it was from the historical circumstances of Christendom, explains how Luther's political theory remained so remarkably unaffected by the tendencies of his time to give independent authority to the German states and to develop political absolutism, and how any church that followed Luther's teaching proved to be defenseless against these tendencies. In historical terms, Barth's judgment on the significance of Luther's doctrine of the two kingdoms does not deal adequately with the circumstances of Luther's era, but it still remains true that the gaps which remained in Luther's synthesis provided the occasion for historical tendencies to take hold in the portion of the Christian tradition influenced by Luther. These were consequences which Luther neither was aware of nor anticipated, and which thus had the historical consequences that Barth and other critics have rightly described as disastrous.

Luther ignored the motifs of a Christian adaptation to and permeation of political thought which have their classical expression in the Byzantine conception of a Christian emperor, and for which the way had been prepared by Origen. This conception was totally different from that which the pre-Christian emperors held of themselves, especially in that the emperor was regarded as a member of the church which was led by bishops, and thus in relation to the spiritual authority vested in the bishops he lacked the self-glorification characteristic of the deified Roman emperors. Anyone who is unable simply to overlook the complex and significant problems affecting the Lutheran doctrine of the two kingdoms, as well as the political traditions of Western Christendom which go back to Augustine, will also be unable to join without further ado in the condemnation so often voiced today of the Eusebian theology of empire, the medieval concept of emperor which was based on it, and the concept of a society—a *corpus Christianum*—whose nature, including structural changes, is determined by Christianity. It is true that this concept cannot be revived today, and that, in addition, in its own day it was so one-sided that it appears inadequate even for the time in which it arose. The self-understanding that the Christian emperors had of themselves as the earthly representatives of Christ's heavenly Kingship made it more or less possible to ignore the eschatological difference between the contemporary political situation in its incompleteness and the future Lordship of God. It was also possible for there to be no consciousness of the actual power of sin in every political order, even one influenced by Christianity, and no fear of God's judgment on sin, even in political life and in the course of history.

Under the deep impression created by Alaric's conquest of Rome, Augustine gave prominence to all these motifs which had been neglected in the Byzantine theology of empire. One was the important concept in the apocalyptic tradition of the contrast between the political kingdoms of this world and the future kingdom of God, which is already present among the righteous, though hidden. Another was the dominance of sin in political life as lust for power and arrogance *(superbia)*, and another the weakness of every present political order under God's judgment on sin in history. But Augustine all too simply put the church in place of the state as the present form of the *civitas Dei*.[18] In Augustine's writings it was no longer the case that the future Kingdom of God corresponded to the political community of the state, and not to the church, nor was it the case that the church and not political life had the nature of a divine ordinance for the interim. Therefore Augustine did not do full justice to the existing positive relationship between political life and the divine sovereignty for which we hope, that is, peace and justice, a relationship that exists despite the eschatologically determined provisional nature of present-day political ordinances and despite the distortion brought about by human sin. His highly significant positive evaluation of political peace is characterized by a tendency that runs counter to the basic idea of his great work, the *City of God,* and it reveals the tension between a dualism derived from apocalyptic and Augustine's lifelong concern that Christian thought should both be integrated with Greek philosophy and go beyond it. Thus Augustine's work is seen to be only partially superior to the Byzantine theology of empire, though superior in its central features. He was only partially able to maintain the positive relationship between justice and peace in the coming reign of God and contemporary political life, and, in addition, he substituted for the identification of the Christian empire with the Lordship of God the no less fatal identification of that Lordship with the church. For these two reasons his work remained in many respects hardly less one-sided than the Eusebian theology of empire.

The limitations of the Lutheran doctrine of two kingdoms are largely due to the influence of Augustinianism. Like Augustine before him, Luther did not do justice to the positive relationship between the hope for the Kingdom of God and the themes of political life, but instead regarded the latter as only an emergency measure against sin. The remarkable detachment of his political principles from the historical situation in which he developed his doctrine marks the difference between Luther and his great model. Augustine's treatise on the *City of God* is largely to be understood as a reworking of the historical experience of his time in theological categories. Luther, however, took account of the historical dimensions of the political situation of his time in his basic thoughts on political order only by ignoring them. This may be due in part to the narrow nature of the relationships among the German territorial states in the sixteenth century. That situation was not favorable to the reworking of the events of Luther's own time in the categories of world history. The isolation of his basic political thought from the contemporary concrete historic experience of Christendom had its historical cause in the late medieval situation in which the independence of the state from the church could be conceived of only by ignoring the given presupposition of a society formed by Christianity, whenever it was a question of the basis of the power of the state. If on the one hand this resulted in the fatal defenselessness of Luther's doctrine against the tendencies of his time toward the autonomy of the theory of the state, it also involved on the other hand his progress beyond Augustine's contrast between the two cities. In Luther's writing, as scarcely anywhere else, we can find a sensitivity to the provisional nature of all merely secular institutions, the church as well as the state, in contrast to the future that brings salvation and God's judgment. Luther can remind us of the fact grounded in eschatology that we cannot surrender the independence of church and state from each other, especially in a society that has been formed and formed anew within the sphere of the Christian tradition. We can also learn from him a commitment to the tasks of the world which goes beyond Augustine and which is motivated by the example of God's love for this world. But nowhere in Luther can we find any inspiration to transform political conditions by the powerful vision of the eschatological Lordship of God which already illumines the present world. This inspiration made its breakthrough elsewhere, in the so-called left wing of the seventeenth century. Here the Christian concept of the freedom of belief made its breakthrough to political freedom and the proud conviction arose that Christians can also take a hand in determining the forms of political life. Luther was close to this insight, which opened the door to the world of ideas of modern democracy. It was finally achieved as the consequence of his concept of the universal priesthood of all believers, that those who believe share both in the priesthood and in the Kingship of Christ. The fact that Luther did not establish this connection, that he did not enter the door to the political thought of the modern world, shows the extent to which his political theory remained dependent on the concerns of the Middle Ages, even though severed from dependence on his historical situation. With his epoch-making renewal of Christian freedom through the immediate relationship of the believer to God, Luther stands at the origins of the political issues of the modern world, but his doctrine of secular force can have significance for us only as a corrective against the fanatical enthusiasm that is so often connected with the idea of freedom.

7

THE NATION AND HUMANITY

Almost six decades ago Friedrich Meinecke described the
development of German political consciousness in terms of the
tension between "world citizenship and the national state." It
appears that after all the catastrophes of our century this theme
has again become timely. In recent years nationalism has often
been pronounced dead. Today it is noticeably alive again, and
already the international ideas and motifs that were the only
meaningful guides for political thought and activity in the
postwar era find their scope narrowed in the name of national
values. Perhaps here we have reached a turning point in
postwar German political thought. In any case it seems
necessary that every citizen for whom political thought is
important rethink his judgments and prejudices on national and
international ideals of political action.

What contribution can the heritage of the Christian tradition
bring to this task? Can we expect that Christian theology has
any contribution to make on this question? We are dealing here
with a question that since the days of the early church has been
closely connected with the central themes of the Christian
tradition. I am speaking expressly of the Christian tradition, not
of Protestant or Catholic doctrine. It seems to me that in the
area of political ethics, just as in other theological questions, we
must overcome the limitations that have hampered the
traditional denominational forms of Christianity. The original
power of biblical motifs has been at work in the history and

traditions of the various Christian churches, and it is vital that it be revealed in all its fullness in the present day. I will therefore not limit myself to the perspectives of the Lutheran doctrine of the two kingdoms, or more accurately, the two ways in which God exercises his Lordship—in the world and in the church. And considerations derived from natural law are just as inadequate a basis for a specifically Christian political ethic. Both ways of looking at the issues provide too little opportunity for specifically Christian motifs to come into play. A Christian political ethic should be permeated by the expectation of the Kingdom of God, God's future Lordship over the world. An approach with this focus would be close to the goal of the Old Testament hope and to the center of the message of Jesus.

Even in the early church there was discussion in the context of the idea of the Kingdom of God concerning whether the precedence should be given to national or international points of view concerning the ordering of political life. I will look at these issues in the first section. In the second section I will evaluate the altered situation, with the contrasts between today's cosmopolitan thinking and the concept of empire in the early church and the Middle Ages. In this connection I will explore the relationships between cosmopolitan and democratic ideas. Or to put it more precisely, I will let the international aspects of the democratic ideas, which embrace all humanity, speak for themselves. In the third section special consideration will be given to the theme of nation and national consciousness from the point of view of an ethic of the Kingdom of God.

I

The age of the official persecutions of Christians in the Roman Empire was not yet at an end when the great Alexandrian theologian Origen set out to overcome the negative attitude of Christians toward the empire. He desired—and was able—to see in the empire of Augustus something more than an offspring of the Antichrist.

Origen applied to Augustus the Messianic words of Ps. 72:7, "In his days may righteousness flourish, and peace abound, till the moon be no more!" He saw in the founding of the empire of Augustus the action of divine providence, which created the earthly preconditions for the universal expansion of the Christian faith: "God was preparing the nations to receive his teachings. They should be subject to the one Roman *basileus*, without the reservation that there are many communities, many nationalities, with no connection with one another."[1] His pagan opponent, the philosopher Celsus, to whom Origen was directing these words, brought against Christian monotheism the reproach that the veneration of only one God produced disorder, because it disrupted the distinctive characteristics of the nations, and it was on their observation and cultivation that the cohesiveness of the Roman Empire depended. In reply, Origen said that on the last day, when God's Kingdom comes, national distinctions will disappear. Because the political achievements of Augustus had already overcome the disunity among the nations, it was working toward the same goal as the Christian message, that is, for the Kingdom of God, which would bring all peoples together.

In the following century Eusebius of Caesarea, contemporary with the great Constantinian transformation, continued and expanded Origen's thought. Building on Luke 2:1, he saw it as the providence of God that Christ appeared at the same time as the setting up of the empire by Augustus. He wrote, "But when our Lord and Savior appeared, and at the same time as his coming, Augustus became the first of the Romans to become lord of the nations, the multiplicity of rulers ended, and peace covered the whole earth."[2] For Eusebius as for Origen the overcoming of national fragmentation and the overcoming of polytheism belonged together. Thus Eusebius could regard Constantine as the one who brought to completion the work which Augustus had begun. Constantine had not only revived the empire of Augustus, but he had combined the political unity of the empire with the exclusive sovereignty of the Christian God.

The theological combination of the universal Christian message with the universal political realm of Constantine and his successors has often been condemned. It has been decried as poor taste to bring the reign of peace, which the prophets foretold, and which was proclaimed as the Kingdom of God, into union with the secular empire of the Romans. But we should remind ourselves that the promise of the coming peaceful reign of God over all the nations had a decisively political significance in the Old Testament. It was expected that the promised Kingdom of God would bring about the fulfillment and completion of political order, an order of justice, in human relationships. In the Kingdom of God the life of humans in community was to find a truly human form. And the hope for the coming Kingdom of God should never be permitted to lose this original political character. If it did, it would be irrelevant for concrete human relationships. And on the other hand the Christian message always unleashed a political force wherever the political meaning of the hope for the Kingdom of God was perceived. Of course the Kingdom of God that Jesus proclaimed is "not of this world" (John 18:36). But it is the future of this world, and Christians have reason for seeing the present world in the light of the future that has been promised to them, and therefore have reason to be on the lookout for transient signs of this hope in the political realm, and to aspire for a provisional realization of it. It has been the distinctive message of Jesus that the coming Kingdom of God as something future is already determining the present. In the light of the originally political nature of the hope for the Kingdom, this must hold true also for political life, and not only for the private life of Christians. And in political life the supreme concern will be the quest for a universal order of peace and justice. Its ultimate realization is the content of the biblical promise of the Lordship of God.

So we can see that the theologians of the early church had good reason for relating the Christian hope for the Kingdom of God to the Roman Empire. And Christians of the present day have every reason to ask which provisional form the Christian hope for a universal order of peace and justice can take in the political situation of the world today. Today as in ancient times there is the danger that the Christian message will be misused to glorify the existing regime. The early church, in its relationship to the Byzantine Empire, did not escape this danger. But the danger can be avoided when in all humility we remain aware that all the ways Christians organize life are at best incomplete and merely temporary in contrast to the final form of the future Kingdom of God. Neither the United States of Europe nor the transformation of the United Nations into an organization that truly transcends national sovereignty with specific supreme laws would finally usher in the Kingdom of God on earth. But it might well be the case that efforts should be made in this direction which would lead to the form of the promised Kingdom of God that, while still temporary, would be its best possible expression in our day. Many of the statements in which John F. Kennedy formulated his vision of a peaceful and just order of human life throughout the entire world contain a reflection of the Old Testament promise of a future kingdom of universal peace. Kennedy's ideas constitute what is perhaps the clearest contemporary expression of a political universalism inspired by Christianity. Nevertheless, as I have said, we are not to do as earlier ages have done and regard the establishment of the Kingdom of God as something that could be achieved by human effort. We must always remain conscious of the fact that every possible Christian way of organizing life remains provisional. This holds true for all "good works," for those in private life as well as for those in public life. Surely Christian humility demands that we not forget the great distance between what we can accomplish and the splendor of the future that God has prepared. Awareness of this distance, however, rightly understood, does not cripple our will to act. On the contrary, awareness of the distance between the promised future of God's kingdom of peace and the circumstances of the present can provide the stimulus to transform the present. The hope for the peaceful kingdom that God has promised can give wings to our imagination and to our will, so that we may overcome whatever there is in the contemporary situation that is regarded as especially inadequate.

II

These last reflections on contemporary possibilities for a political universalism inspired by Christianity make the tacit assumption that the promised Kingdom of God, with its peace and justice, can no longer take on for us today the political form of world monarchy. Such a monarchy was for the early Christians the earthly copy of God's Lordship over the world. But there is an unavoidable ambiguity in monarchical rule—seen in theological terms—in that the monarch must be seen as a rival of God's rule as well as its representative, inasmuch as he is the highest earthly authority; beyond whom there is no other authority to which appeal can be made. Jesus Christ is the Messiah, the representative of God's Lordship over humanity, because he did not seek for or exercise human lordship, but rather for the sake of the proclamation of God's Lordship delivered himself up to death on the cross. Thus through Jesus Christ the contrast between ruler and ruled is overcome. It is overcome for Christians because they are united with Jesus Christ through faith, baptism, and the Lord's Supper. In this way they share in his priestly office as well as in his royal office. For this reason, monarchy, at least absolute monarchy, with its distinction in principle between ruler and ruled, is not appropriate for Christianity. Just as there is the universal priesthood of all believers, so there is also their universal kingship. In historical and doctrinal terms, this idea contains the Christian roots of modern democracy.

To be sure, modern democracy goes back not only to Christian roots, but to classical roots as well. Equality and freedom of all full citizens were the basis of ancient Greek democracy. Stoic philosophers were the first to acknowledge that all humans as humans had the right to freedom and equality. But Greek history seems to teach that democratic constitutions cannot endure, because the citizens were not able to attain to the necessary unity of purpose. As a result, it seemed that political order could be achieved only through the rule of a single individual. Equality and freedom were the marks of a golden age of mankind, now unfortunately far in the past.

In a manner similar to that of Stoic thought, Christian theology regarded human freedom and equality as properties of our original nature, which, however, had been lost in the Fall and would be attained again only in the future felicity of the Kingdom of God. For the mainstream of Christian theology, as for Stoic philosophy, freedom and equality belong to our basic humanity, but they have been lost by the corruption of mankind. For Christianity, however, freedom and equality are not only connected with a golden age of the distant past; they are also to be present in the future in which God will again bring to realization the equality of all humans. And in Christian theology there was the further possibility of bringing the glorious future of mankind into play for the present, for the sake of the fellowship of Christians with Christ, who is the new man, the true human being.[3] Thus Christian faith made it possible to take two decisive steps beyond Stoic thought. Not only were humans once free and equal in the past, but they will be so again, and it is not necessary to wait for the distant future for this to be the case. Humans are able even in the present to draw on their human nature and destiny, for their fellowship with Christ enables them to rise above the limitations of their present existence and of their own weakness.

The universal nature of the Christian hope for a political order of peace and justice that would unite all humanity has the closest connection with democratic ideals. This is true first of all of the democratic principles. They are based on humans as humans, on all humans, not on the people of this or that nation. Thus from the outset the concept of world citizenship is a vital part of democratic thought. Many pioneers in the struggle for democratic ideals have also expected that democratic institutions would result in the disappearance of the differences and the distinctions among nations and in a tendency of all members of the human race to grow closer to each other. Today we know that this tendency will not automatically attain its goal. Even a democratic state can fall victim to nationalism, and the result can be a hatred of other nations to a degree unknown in earlier times. The human pathos of democratic ideals needs to be united with the goal of establishing a peaceful order that will embrace all mankind. By the same token, the hope for world peace contains features that can come to full development only in a society where there are freedom and equality. The promised kingdom of peace is expected to bring about a social structure in which the true humanity of all will be acknowledged. The Kingdom of God that was hoped for in the Old Testament was symbolized in The Book of Daniel by a human form, in order to distinguish between the nature of its rule and the violent rule of the great empires, which were symbolized by animal forms. I have already stressed that the Lordship of Christ puts an end to all rule by violence, because by the cross of Christ and the sacramental union of Christ with those who believe in him, the contrast between ruler and ruled is overcome. Even the early church was convinced that the full realization of our humanity in the Kingdom of God would do away with all distinctions of origin and of social position. To this extent Christian theology was right in seeing in the Stoic concepts of the original freedom and equality of all humans something with which it had close affinity. It adapted these Stoic ideas and transformed them into a promise for the future of mankind.

The Christian adaptation of the Stoic ideas changed the meaning of freedom and equality and, consequently, the basis of democracy. For Stoic thought, freedom and equality are a part of original human nature, and thus for the Stoic they are attributes of present-day humans, in spite of all the inequality that has arisen in the course of history; humans are essentially equal and equally free, if we are able to cut through the differences that have been brought about by society.[4] Christianity, however, does not regard the differences among humans as something unreal in contrast to the actual features that all have in common. Those differences are insignificant only in comparison with the common destiny of humans to enjoy community in the Kingdom of God. Christianity does not understand humans as equal and equally free in that which they already are, but as called to a freedom and equality before God, which is not yet present, but in which they believe. Democratic ideals are easy to criticize when they are interpreted in the Stoic sense of an already existing equality and freedom. This equality is only the leveling out of all differences, not only differences of origin and possessions, but also those of gifts and accomplishments. And wherever this abstract equality of humans is made the standard of political action, serious injustice, that is, the leveling down of everything that is special and distinguished, can hardly be avoided.

The Christian concept of equality does not mean that everyone is to be reduced to an average where every voice is equal to every other, but equality in the Christian sense means that everyone should be raised up through participation in the highest human possibilities. Such equality must always be created; it is not already there. And it can be created only through the power of brotherhood. This is the third basic word of modern democracy, and the one that has the clearest Christian roots, but it is all too easy to forget in comparison with freedom and equality. But it is the power of brotherhood, the power of creative love, that alone is able to bind different persons together in community and, with this community, to bring about an equality that was not previously present. Brotherhood must help individuals to overcome the limits of their present existence, so that they can be free to achieve their common human destiny. Brotherhood means giving each person a genuine chance to participate fully in all the opportunities of the society. Abraham Lincoln saw this as the real meaning of the concept of equality.[5] Everyone is not equal and cannot be treated as if equal, but everyone can and must be given a true chance to attain the same goals. This idea of Lincoln's that everyone must be given a chance makes clear what it means to speak of an equality that must first be brought about.[6]

The discussion so far has shown that the universal idea of humanity, which is particularly indebted to the Christian ethic of the Kingdom of God, not only has an "external political" relevance for the struggle for a peaceful order of humanity that would encompass all the nations; it also has an "internal political" guiding power, because it is concerned with democratic ideals about humans as such. But a democratic community cannot at the outset include all humanity. It has to develop in the life together and in the political institutions of a specific people, in the realm of a limited political state. Thus we cannot avoid any longer the question of the role of the national community in the context of an ethic of the Lordship of God. Only in this context, however, is it possible for the nation to become a theme of a Christian ethic that is faithful to its task. That is why we are only now coming back, after exploring the democratic idea of humanity, to the phenomenon of the nation. Even so it is not at all easy to grasp why it was possible to identify Christianity and fatherland, as can be illustrated by so many instances from history.

III

National governments seem always to have become the direct political partners of the Christian churches whenever the Christian hope for the Kingdom of God found no corresponding expression in political life or when the concept of the Kingdom of God was so altered that no more attempts were made to seek a political reality that could be considered its expression. For Western Europe both of these events came about for the first time late in the ancient world. The Roman Empire, at least its western part, collapsed under the assaults of the great migrations, and at the same time the concept of the Kingdom of God became depoliticized.

The two developments are connected. It was the weakness of the Byzantine theology of empire, as it later was of that of the medieval period, that the Christian *imperium* as the earthly representative of the Kingdom of God was regarded as indestructible. This led the church to forget the critical function which the Christian hope for the future had toward all present social structures. As a result, the provisional and perishable nature of the Roman Empire made an even greater impression on the people when the Western Empire fell. It was then easy to abandon, along with the absolute Byzantine theology of empire, every connection between the hope for the Kingdom of God and political life. Augustine expressed the historical experience of his era when he contrasted the Kingdom of God and secular political structures.[7]

Thus Augustine became the defender of a doctrine of two kingdoms. And we can see here that in such an understanding the difference between the Kingdom of God and all human political structures finds clear expression, but also that this difference remains unfruitful, because the sundering of the two realms results in a situation in which the Kingdom of God no longer is a critical force that can overcome the limitations of the given political situation. Augustine did not entirely relegate the Kingdom of God to a realm beyond history. He separated it from politics only to find it embodied in the church, which stood unshaken amid all the disorder of his age.

The uniting of Kingdom of God and church had far-reaching historical consequences. First, the church of the early Middle Ages felt that it was the heir of the Roman Empire as the sole universal institution of Christendom. In the political realm it saw itself confronted only by the various peoples.[8] As a theory for the way the church worked together with the political powers within Christianity, there developed the concept of "two powers," the secular and the spiritual. In this way the secular force, whose task was to serve the Kingdom of God by preserving peace and righteousness, no longer needed to be a world empire. In its struggle against the claims of the medieval emperors the church could ally itself with the national states against the concept of a universal secular order in Christendom. Following the collapse of imperial power, the Catholic Church once again filled the role of the sole universal institution of Christianity in contrast to the particularism of the nations, and has so continued to the present.

That is one form of the relationship of the church to the national states. The other is encountered in Luther's theory of the two kingdoms, or in its successors. This doctrine also goes back to the medieval theory of the two powers, but for Luther the spiritual power of the church is no longer represented by a universal institution. Consequently the danger was particularly great that the church would become dependent on the territorial powers and later on the nation states.

Luther stood in the tradition of the Augustinian doctrine of two kingdoms to the extent that he no longer regarded political life in the light of the hope for the Kingdom of God. Consequently the theological meaning of a universal political order as at least a temporary form of God's promised kingdom of peace was not something he thought about. Otherwise he would not have been able simply to accept the many territorial states, the precursors of the later national states, as the normal form of secular authority. This was a highly questionable step. Many advantages may be seen in Luther's doctrine of the two kingdoms: It points out clearly the difference between the Kingdom of God and present political reality, as well as the difference between church and state. And it is not true that it led Christians to take a merely passive attitude toward political power. But the difference between the Kingdom of God and the current political situation was no longer able to create a dynamic for change in contemporary situations. Instead, the field of political activity was abandoned to powers that felt no duty, as the Christian empire had because of its own nature, to honor Christian goals. To be sure, there were statesmen who were motivated by Christian ideals, but the political interests of the regional states of the sixteenth century, and especially of the later national states, had little to do with Christian motifs or goals. Herein lay the problem of Luther's doctrine of the two kingdoms.

There is no need to describe here in more detail how the theory on which the territorial states were based moved away from Christian motifs and goals. Instead we must focus our attention on the contradiction between Christendom and modern nationalism, even though that does not exhaust the phenomenon of the nation in the light of a Christian political ethic. The modern elevation of the nation as the dominant model of political action is in clear contradiction to the international traditions of Christianity and to their source in the Christian hope that all humans may participate in the Kingdom of God. This is especially obvious in the way that nationalism used biblical ideas to express its self-image, resulting in the perversion of biblical ideas to deify the nation and its people. Thus the concept of the chosen people was applied to modern nations such as England or Germany in order to provide them with the prestige of a religious mission. But the tendency to think of one's own people as chosen by God, in analogy to ancient Israel, misinterpreted the uniqueness of Israel for salvation history, which was expressed by Israel's designation as God's chosen people. Moreover, the purpose for which God chose his people was to win all humanity to the God of Israel. In principle this goal was attained in Jesus Christ and in the world Christian mission, insofar as the transition was made from the choosing of one people to the calling of all mankind to partake in Christian salvation. From then on the concept of a chosen people represented a falling away from the Christian concern with all mankind. The nationalistic secularization of this idea must therefore be condemned as anti-Christian.

It is no accident that in modern times the idea of nation has contributed to the elimination of Christian motifs from the formation of political consciousness. When national interests are the guiding star of the state and politics, we find ourselves in a sphere where the Christian expectation of the Kingdom of God as a time of peace and justice for all mankind is indeed foreign. The Christian churches have not recognized clearly enough or taken seriously enough the resulting alienation of political life from the spirit of Christianity. To be sure, the churches were by no means thoroughly involved in the cult of the nation, not even in Germany.[9] But they did not know how to overcome the narrowness of nationalistic thought by establishing far-reaching political goals and thus to bring it into relation to the worldwide horizon of Christian hope. The churches accommodated themselves to nationalism in the spirit of the theory of the two powers. They should have felt themselves called, if anyone did, to oppose a development that led to the mutual mangling of the nations of Europe in the name of insane nationalistic ideas.

It cannot be claimed that this development was only the consequence of avoidable exaggerations of national spirit. Recently such opinions have been frequently encountered.[10] I fear that they tend to depict the true state of affairs as harmless. Wherever the nation becomes the focus of political thought, there must inevitably arise a struggle for preeminence. Even the romantic forerunners of German nationalism did not preach hatred of other peoples but believed in a harmonious coexistence of the nations. Yet even so their ideas led not only to cultural competition among the nations but also to a struggle for political power, and then to the struggle for dominance. That harmonious coexistence of the nations which inspired Herder and Schleiermacher is possible on a permanent basis only in the context of comprehensive goals and international institutions.

All this does not mean that Christian political ethics should deny any significant role to the nation in political thought and action. Belonging to the same nation because of a common language, common culture, common historical experience, or a combination of all these factors is without doubt a historical fact that as such demands attention, and that no one can simply ignore. It is important to endeavor to attain clarity about it one way or another. As the obvious analogy for national identity, the idea of the extended family claims our attention, but it has been less subject to the influence of historical changes than has the nation. The theological ethics of the previous century generally regarded "people" and also "family" as God's "ordinances of creation." This concept has many aspects. First, it is a theological expression of the fact that there are nations in existence and that each person finds himself or herself living in the context of a people. Beyond this, however, the concept of ordinances of creation is intended to serve as a basis for the duties the individual owes to the family or to the people. Here the issues become clear. The concept of an ordinance of creation is unable to establish a specific relationship between the nation and specifically Christian ideas. For this reason, if for no other, it is cause for concern that what is said about "people" as an ordinance of creation is intended to go beyond the acceptance of the existence of nations, and to derive from their existence a specific obligation for its citizens. The mere existence of a people is no basis at all for the contention that the preservation of national distinctions is the will of God. The extent and nature of nations have changed too often in the course of history. Peoples have perished and others have arisen. The mere fact of an existing national unit cannot provide the basis of an "imperative to loyalty to the people" that would be binding on those who comprise the people.[11] Consequently the interpretation of the fact of national identity by the concept of an ordinance of creation is highly questionable, especially since it has proved to be susceptible to nationalistic abuse.

The Christian hope for the coming Kingdom of God casts additional light on the fact that people belong to a particular nation. The joint participation of all humans in a kingdom of peace and righteousness cannot be directly attained through a worldwide collection of individuals. It is possible only as a society of various larger groups, which again represent the unity of smaller groups. The development and preservation of a consciousness of belonging together wherever common factions are present is the only way to establish larger political units. It is not isolated individuals but the groups that they form that can join together in larger societies. In this sense national identity has a positive significance as an unavoidable step toward larger human communities. It also provides the criterion that sets limits on national egoism.

From this point of view we can understand the rightness of the demand for national states that inspired the national movements of the preceding century. The rightness of this demand does not result from those things which the citizens of a nation have in common, but from the claim to political self-determination based on human dignity, in terms of freedom and equality as our human destiny. In addition it must be said that the demand for a national state cannot have the status of a basic principle which was accorded to it earlier. A state comprising various nationalities, such as the old Austro-Hungarian Empire, is not of necessity something that can be rejected in every circumstance. This insight cannot be displeasing to those whom the task of building political communities points beyond the interests of their own nation.

The interpretation of national identity as a step toward larger human communities enables us to cultivate national characteristics, our own language, culture, and customs. A comprehensive political unity will hold together better through a multiplicity of mutually supplementary distinctive traits than it will through uniformity. But the cultivation of the distinctive features has meaning only insofar as it makes a contribution to the life of the whole.

Above all, however, the cultivation of national distinctions must be subordinated to the concern for an international order of justice and freedom. Harmony among the nations does not come about of itself, as our experience has shown. Therefore international federations will be most successful if they begin with limited groupings, based on a common history and culture, as well as on common political and economic interests. In our own time the progress of European integration is an outstanding example of such confederations. Such unions of nations, however, should be oriented beyond their own bounds toward the idea of an order of justice and peace that should one day include all humanity, that is, not only the world of our friends but also our present enemies. Thus this sequence of specific unions, which must have their beginning in the internal political life of each people that is involved, and in which the national community then finds its proper place, points toward the universal goal of a peaceful world that encompasses all mankind. Because of its connection with the biblical expectation of the Kingdom of God, this concept must be the criterion of any Christian political ethic. Applied as a criterion it implies, for example, that the idea of a united Europe has its full ethical authority only when a united Europe does not close itself off against the rest of the world, and when it knows how to portray the humanity in its own culture and democratic order in such a way that it will have the power to attract the rest of mankind. For the national problems of Germany, this criterion of the biblical expectation of the Kingdom of God means that our national interests must be dealt with not as ends in themselves, but only in the context of overarching goals, the foremost of which is and remains European unity. This context with its comprehensive political goals of European unity and world peace determines the boundary between the justifiable cultivation of distinctive national features and nationalistic exaggerations.

At this point allow me to put things a little more concretely. No German political policy can abandon the concern for a new political realization of our national solidarity with the millions of Germans beyond the Elbe. That the form of this political community must be the result of the free self-determination of the German people is a stipulation that is derived from human dignity, in terms of our destiny to be free and equal human beings. In addition, this condition will be effective to the degree to which human destiny is realized in a more convincing manner in this part of Germany. On the other hand it seems to me that the demand for the restoration of Germany's borders as they were before 1937 can be advanced only from a rather abstract standpoint of national rights. Is the Polish population living today beyond the Oder and Neisse Rivers to be resettled again? If so, where to? Should we expect the Soviet Union to return the old eastern districts of Poland?[12] These are clearly unreal expectations, and the survival of such goals in parts of the West German population should not be given any official encouragement. I am saying this in the national interest. Our stiff-necked clinging to unattainable goals could well lead us into a situation where we might forfeit for a long time to come goals that may still be attainable, even though by many detours, goals such as political unity with the people of East Germany. Without reaching an understanding with our East European neighbors, especially with Poland, this urgent national concern can have no prospect of fulfillment at all. It is said again and again that all territorial settlements should be delayed until a peace treaty is concluded. But who can say that after twenty years there is still any hope for the conclusion of a treaty of peace? Does not such a treaty become more superfluous with each passing year? Our policy toward the East will make clear in the long run the degree to which German political policy is ready to incorporate national aspirations into a comprehensive conception that embraces all Europe and to subordinate them to the demands of mankind. Or will our policy, for the sake of certain national principles, lead us to close our eyes to the situation brought about by the end of the war, which by all human estimates can scarcely be revised? It is probably not always possible for the holders of political office in our country to discuss this question openly. All the more then is it the duty of the rest of our citizens to do so, because only in this way can an atmosphere be created in which a German government will one day have the freedom to take the appropriate action.

It is said again and again that we Germans of today lack a national consciousness. That is quite correct. But the basis of this lack is the lack of clarity concerning our present political situation. A free German national consciousness, free of nationalistic exaggeration, can develop only when we determine to stop excluding from our consciousness the consequences of the war for the eastern part of our land. Only then will a German be able to speak the word "fatherland" without worrying that he is thereby becoming involved in a political adventure whose outcome is unpredictable. To be sure, even then the fatherland must never again become the highest value in our political thought and action. Without being led astray by the ups and downs of daily politics we must hold fast to the goal of a European unity that will be more than a "Europe of Fatherlands," and beyond that goal we must make our contribution to a future that will bring a better provision for the peace of mankind. A policy that is directed toward this universal goal and in the service of the universal destiny of mankind seeks to provide occasion for all to live together in peace as well as for the training of one's own citizens in freedom and equality. Such a policy may with justification claim to draw its strength from the best roots of the Christian tradition. It is probable that at the same time it would also best meet the national aspirations of our people.

8

THE PEACE OF GOD
AND WORLD PEACE

Under the pressure of the concern for world peace, talk of peace in any but directly political terms will seem futile today, a diversion from the urgent task on which all our energy and insight must be concentrated. To turn one's attention to peace with God, especially in the sense of peace of soul, can easily give the impression of cynicism or bigotry in view of the terror which threatens the future of mankind in the atomic age. Nonetheless, peace with God may have more to do with world peace than a superficial glance would indicate. It could prove to be a source of strength that enables the ordinary citizen to exert new efforts for peace and not give in to resignation, thinking that peace will finally be preserved—or lost—only by those who wield power on earth.

Truthfulness requires us to acknowledge that the peace of God about which the New Testament speaks is not identical with world peace. Such divine peace far excels everything that can be understood as world peace. If world peace involves the progressive limitation, or, if possible, the renunciation of the use of armed force by the individual states in the waging of international conflict, then the peace of God is concerned with the well-being, the wholeness of our existence, a wholeness which in this life is found only in fragmentary form. It cannot be produced by our efforts; it can become present only by grace, in the midst of all that is provisional, and as a foreshadowing, in the midst of the suffering of everyday life, of complete peace. By contrast, world peace, which must take the form of a political condition, is something entirely provisional and is by no means either present salvation or a golden age. In addition, the peace of God in the New Testament writings is promised to the Christian church or to individuals. This promise is almost always made in reference to the relationships of persons to one another, and without explicit reference to the task of bringing about political and military peace between peoples and nations. This naturally does not mean that the peace which comes from the divine Jesus, and of which Colossians says that it is "peace by the blood of the cross of Christ" (Col. 1:20), has nothing at all to do with the political aspects of peace. This dimension is part of the background of the New Testament statements about peace. Whenever peace is mentioned or described in the great prophetic promises of final salvation in the Old Testament, it involves peace among the nations. To be sure, this is not a matter of limiting the use of force in international conflicts, a step toward the realization of peace in the world, but a matter of overcoming the conflicts which are the occasion of violent encounters. The ending of such conflicts is anticipated as the result of the universal worship of Yahweh and of following the laws that he has established. Worldwide peace, together with justice, which is inseparable from it, is the most important mark of that long-awaited divine Lordship which will one day replace the forms of authority exercised by the empires of this world. It is in the light of such prophetic promises that we are to understand the message of Jesus that God's Kingdom is at hand, and everything that the New Testament writings say about the peace of God. If in the light of the divine secret, humans are to become whole, thus winning salvation and attaining peace in the full meaning of the word, then the political dimension of human destiny must be taken into account. God's Lordship, which makes it possible for human life to become whole, includes political peace. This concept is in the background of the New Testament statements about peace, but no emphasis is placed on it. This situation can be explained at least in part by the fact that for the Judea of that day the only alternative to insurrection against the Roman occupation was political resignation. It is understandable that in this situation the Pax Romana was not regarded as the fulfillment of the Old Testament prophecies of peace. This connection was made only later, although it is foreshadowed in Luke. Still the major reason for the scarcity of references to the concept of political peace in the New Testament must be sought elsewhere. Even for Luke the accomplishment of the kingdom of universal peace promised by the prophets does not commence in the political realm but begins with one individual, Jesus. Through him the peace of God was already present for the early church in the small groups of those who believed in him. Only the letter to the Ephesians (2:14-22) specifically states that this peace of God involves all mankind. The cross of Christ, by abolishing the law, has brought about peace between Jews and Gentiles. The prophetic promises of peace on the one hand and the universal mission of Christians to all mankind on the other hand determine the scope of this early Christian understanding of peace.

How are we to understand the statement that the cross of Jesus has brought the peace which the prophets foretold? Ephesians apparently means that the cross of Jesus Christ has broken through those claims of Jewish religion which excluded Gentiles. This may perhaps be broadened into the general statement that the cross of Christ breaks through the claims to truth that humans make against each other, and that it thereby brings peace, so that humans learn to recognize the provisional nature of all movements that separate them from one another. The way in which the cross accomplishes this needs to be explained in more profound terms. We must first of all consider the causes of that lack of peace so characteristic of daily human life. There are fleeting moments in which we realize the fullness and richness of our existence, but in everyday life we are driven by care and haste. In our striving for self-assertion and security, time runs through our fingers, and the older we become the faster it runs. Thus we become separated from that inexpressible depth in all that is real, the depth that is also the power which is over all. The life that we lead becomes a struggle against God. We express no gratitude to him. Yet these efforts to secure our existence individually and collectively and to succeed in our competition against others cannot be easily avoided. They are necessary because our life is constantly threatened by encroachment and danger. But behind each new danger and encroachment that threatens our happiness there waits death, which finally overtakes us all. Anyone who does not live a life of thankfulness to God is defenseless against the anxiety of death, and in this anxiety lies the deepest reason for the lack of peace in our existence. Only in the light of this situation does it become clear how great the peace is which the death of Jesus brought, and what kind of peace it is. He brought peace to all humans who are united to him by overcoming death, which robs our existence of tranquillity. By his death he gave us a hope that goes beyond death, because our fellowship with him also assures us of participation in the life of his resurrection from the dead. Therefore Paul could speak of the peace with God which we have through faith in Jesus Christ (Rom. 5:1), and this Pauline idea may be the basis of the application of Christ's death to the relationship of Jews and Gentiles as set forth in Ephesians (2:13-18). Everyone who, freed from the fear of death, has peace with God can withstand all the limits placed on human claims, even his own.

It is important for the Christian concept of peace, including its effect on political ethics, to remember that the peace of God, which Jesus brought, is based on the overcoming of death and is made available to us precisely through the death of Jesus. By this means, and only by this means, is there peace in the midst of suffering, amid the injustice and anxiety of this world. This is why the peace instituted by Jesus' death and resurrection can become a source of peace for the world. It must be said with all clarity, however, that the peace of God, which is available to mankind through Jesus, remains firm even if we do not succeed in securing and preserving world peace. Even through the horrors of a nuclear war, the peace of God in Christ would not become a farce; on the contrary, even then, especially then, it would be the final hope of the suffering and dying.

This does not make commitment to the cause of world peace superfluous but motivates such commitment. Anyone who, here and now, does not work wherever possible for peace among mankind, even in the face of the danger that it could all be in vain, has no share in the peace of God which has been made available to mankind through the death and resurrection of Jesus. What might be considered peace of soul for the isolated individual who no longer feels responsible for his fellow humans and for society bears more resemblance to self-satisfied sloth than to the peace of God. The challenge is to take part in the incarnational movement of the coming of God, which Jesus proclaimed and which took place when through him the hope for the future Kingdom of God and its peace became present reality. Since God desires peace now in the midst of the turmoil of the world, Jesus could praise the peacemakers and say they will be called children of God (Matt. 5:9). God recognizes them as belonging to him, because through them the same spirit is at work who speaks through the action of God in sending Jesus into the world—the spirit of peace for this world that suffers so much from the absence of peace. Only those who let themselves be moved by the spirit of peace share in the peace of God. The blessing given to the peacemakers therefore was not originally directed only to the disciples; rather, the unlimited scope of the beatitude applied to everyone who works for peace. Everyone who works in this way is filled with the spirit of God which Jesus announced, whether he confesses himself a Christian or not. This is the basis for cooperation between Christians and non-Christians everywhere where peace is at stake, whether it is a matter of domestic peace, the common good, which in the Bible always involves justice, or whether it is working for the limitation of armaments, which we want to see achieved in the interests of world peace.

For the Christian there is therefore a "drive toward peace," and not only in the sense that the renunciation of the use of nuclear weapons and the institutional anchoring of such renunciation in our present age of advancing technology has become a condition for survival. For the Christian the commitment to peace goes beyond this, as a matter of faithfulness to the spirit of the gospel. In this sense too there is for the Christian a "drive toward peace." It is not possible to be a Christian without helping to preserve peace and working in one's own circle in the interests of peace.

The history of Christianity provides a dismaying commentary on such observations. It has certainly not been less filled with wars than the history of other cultures, but has exceeded their record, especially in recent centuries. If we seek the reasons for this, they are certainly not to be found exclusively in a failure of the Christian will for peace. As Christians assumed responsibility for political leadership in the Roman Empire, they could not long avoid the task of securing the internal peace of the empire against external threats, in spite of reservations about the compatibility of waging war and their position as Christians.

This should not be regarded on principle and in each individual case as a departure from the spirit of the gospel, unless we intend to forbid Christians to take part in political life at all. That would contradict the political significance of the Old Testament promises of peace, which set the stage for the New Testament's message of peace. And Christians who as a matter of principle reject the dirty work of politics and the use of armed force find themselves in the ambiguous position of being beneficiaries of those who take such tasks on themselves on behalf of the entire society, and thus also on behalf of Christians. Nonetheless the decision of individuals and even several entire Christian communities not to participate in the exercise of force by the government has symbolic meaning for all Christendom. This could not, however, serve as the only, universal answer to the demand to undertake political responsibility without denying the claims which the coming

Lordship of God makes on each present age, even in the political realm. It goes without saying that Christians who are active in politics, insofar as they understand their political activity as confirmation of their Christian identity, are involved in the tensions of the political struggle for peace. This certainly was the case in earlier times. It would be wrong to reject wholesale such efforts on the part of Christians of earlier generations. Solutions could not always be achieved, because in many cases the situation did not allow things to turn out differently.

But neither should we be willing to grant wholesale justification to the bellicose history of Christianity. The worst thing is not that the history of Christianity has been marked by wars that broke all restraints and violated all principles of morality and international law. Worse than that is the fact that wars were waged that made false use of the name Christian, and out of false missionary zeal sought to spread the faith in the one who was crucified, who taught and lived love for his enemies. And wars were waged out of dogmatic impatience in the name of the one who said, "Blessed are the meek." This was possible only because of a church orthodoxy that arrogated to its own insights the finality of the Kingdom of God. By this the church missed the opportunity to make room for the future Lordship of God in this world which is not yet the Kingdom of God but which is directed forward by the message of God's future beyond the limits of the present, even the present of its ecclesiastical existence. In the wars of religion at the time of the Reformation, just as earlier during the Crusades and the wars against heretics, there were appalling violations of the spirit of the gospel. But in the same way as the use of military force in the name of the gospel brought suffering, the opposite alternative, the liberation of the state from the demands of the gospel, plunged the people of Christendom into unspeakable misfortune, especially through the belief that the nation was the highest political good, a belief that arose to fill the vacuum that had been left. The *reductio ad absurdum* of this belief was provided by the two world wars of our century, in which the peoples of European Christendom butchered each other, and there are even now persons who are unwilling to learn the lesson that is to be drawn from those wars. The same might be said for the theological distinction between the two realms in which God rules, the state as the ordinance of preservation and the church as the ordinance of redemption. This doctrine gives expression to a widespread tendency in the modern world to separate religion and politics, which resulted in granting autonomy to the territorial states and thereby later prepared the way for the rise of nationalism. This tendency helped bring about a situation in which Christianity in modern times merely served to sanction systems of government that had their origins elsewhere.

As a result of the intolerance of the religious wars and because of the failure of Christians to participate in politics, the churches of the world missed their chance to testify to the political relevance of the gospel's message of peace. The causes of the sterility of Christian thinking about peace in the history of Christianity may well reside on the one hand in the dogmatism and in the intolerance that it has produced, and on the other in the isolation of a self-satisfied spiritual realm where an inner religiosity is cultivated.

Today the danger of wars of faith, at least under the sign of Christianity, seems no longer real. To be sure, in the 1950s there was still the possibility that the cold war waged for the Christian West against atheistic Communism might be continued in armed conflict under a similar sign. We can hope that time is now past, but the other danger is all the greater. The inherited separation of religion and politics maintains itself tenaciously in the public consciousness, thus weakening the awareness of a Christian mission to work for peace, even in the realm of politics. The insight must be more widely shared that we are dealing not with a situation that can be turned over to the professional politicians but with a basic problem of Christian identity, with faithfulness to the spirit of the gospel.

This does not mean that it is a question of bringing about the peace of God and with it God's Lordship by direct political means. Whoever bears in mind that the peace of God means the wholeness of being and the presence of that salvation which overcomes all sorrow and calms all anxiety and insecurity, and whoever remembers that the peace of God which was made accessible through Jesus is therefore involved with victory over death, will not easily get the idea that it would be possible to bring about that final well-being of the peace of God under the form of some new political movement. Wherever such claims are made, it is, as a rule, the case that the accompanying intolerance displays the features of the Antichrist. The political action of Christians can contribute only in a provisional way to the resolution of the conflicts that break out again and again in the world in which we live, in the play of political forces as well as in interpersonal relationships. The task of the peacemaker, then, does not demand that we distance ourselves from conflicts or repress them, but that we disarm them and settle them. That task means that at all levels we will take precautions to prevent existing conflicts from developing into destructive clashes. The conflicts themselves, insofar as they are expressions of the clash of conflicting interests, can seldom simply be eliminated, but they can be reduced in intensity so that a clash is avoided until the critical phase is past.

In this sense a contribution can be made to peace, even to world peace, not only by governments but also by each individual. It can come about through formation of public opinion concerning the necessity of peace and of the conditions that promote it. Only seldom can public opinion force governments to take specific actions, but especially in a democracy it can make it easier or more difficult for a government to make a specific political decision. Naturally public opinion is in turn significantly influenced by the positions taken by governments or parties, but there are also other influences at work, and each individual can contribute to this process. The Christian churches too, and such institutions as this *Kirchentag*, are involved in the formation of public opinion. The possible significance of such contributions to the formation of opinion can be illustrated by the remarkable improvement in German political policy toward Eastern Europe in the past year. It is doubtful that this change in the direction of a realistic concern for mutual understanding would have been psychologically possible without the Protestant memorandum concerning those peoples who have been forcibly resettled, and parallel concerns, such as the exchange of correspondence between the German and Polish bishops. As a result of such actions, a decade-old taboo was broken, and the mere fact of public discussion on the subject means that the taboo no longer seems obvious. This in turn would not have been possible if the discussion over the memorandum had not aroused widespread discontent with the unrealistic character of earlier policy toward Eastern Europe. This can serve as a model case for studying the possible effects of efforts toward influencing public opinion. Similar action can and must be taken in the interest of the more comprehensive theme of securing the peace. The memorandum of the Protestant Church and similar efforts have cast light on one aspect of the problem. Without genuine reconciliation with Germany's neighbors in Eastern Europe, peace in Europe remains uncertain. The memorandum, by speaking out for such reconciliation, also implicitly opposed nationalism, which among us as elsewhere is one of the greatest hindrances to international peace.

Such reconciliation would place limits on the sovereignty of the national states and on their other special interests that drive them remorselessly forward on a collision course. This is a direction in which we must further explore the question of the chances for peace and the obstacles in its way. There is a growing revival, among us as well as elsewhere, of nationalism as the benchmark of all political thought and action. We must clearly recognize that nationalism as a political principle is contrary to the development of a worldwide peaceful order. We do not need a new national consciousness, as we recently have so often heard claimed, but we need a consciousness of the tasks incumbent on our people within the framework of the European community and of a human race, the major portion of which does not have even today the economic conditions for human dignity. We need, not a new national consciousness, but a clear awareness of the demands of the one world in which humanity must live tomorrow and which now can be realized only in the framework of global peace, whether brought about by institutions or existing de facto. We must take more interest in the question of how the material conditions of life can be assured tomorrow for a world population that grows at an alarming rate, so that we may avoid desperate conflicts between the poor and the rich. We must gird ourselves for the economic sacrifice that we will have to make as one of the rich nations of this earth, and we must be prepared to make this sacrifice if we succeed in organizing assistance for economic development in a sensible and effective manner. This could come about if such aid were transferred from a national basis to international institutions, as William Fulbright, the American senator, has suggested. In this way aid for development could be freed from any ambiguous connection with the political and economic interests of the donor nations. Such an internationalized organization for development could through its own weight become an element in the integration of humanity. It could make a contribution to the growth of world peace that would not necessarily have to be based on treaties, as long as it functioned effectively in reality. Its chances seem highly uncertain, not only because of the opposition of the world powers but also in the light of unlimited population growth, especially in many developing countries.

The Christian churches have a clear responsibility to work toward a peaceful future for mankind. In the present world situation no one can any longer take comfort from the idea that the interests of all mankind can be best served by one or the other of the great powers. After the hopes of the Kennedy era, the Vietnam War constituted for many the painful lesson that the United States of America, in spite of its great political tradition, found its intentions that were directed toward the well-being of mankind defeated by power politics—the "Arrogance of Power," as Senator Fulbright termed it. Fulbright showed that this reversal resulted from a fixation on ideological opposition to communism. This opposition needs to be overcome by the concept of humankind as a community of sovereign and independent nations. A community of sovereign nations, today, however, can be protected from destruction through the collision of national interests only if there is a willingness to limit sovereignty in the interests of world peace. Christians must contribute to making it easier for their governments to take steps toward such world peace by bringing to bear the force of public opinion. Even though this will not bring in the final peaceful reign of God, it can still be the firstfruits of that peace in the world politics of the present day.

How should we picture this peaceful society for which we are striving? There would be genuine security against the outbreak of war only if there were an international institution that could force all nations, including the great powers, to maintain the peace, that is, one that would have military superiority over the great powers. Therefore many hold that such an institution, which by the exercise of power would take on the nature of a supreme world government, is the only way out of the dilemma of the atomic age. But in the present world situation it is inconceivable that the great powers would renounce the use of their nuclear weapons in the interests of such an institution. More than that, it is a major question how such an institution could be prevented from abusing its power when there was no longer any power that could place limitations on it. This casts doubt on the desirability of a central international power of this sort and leaves us with the question whether mankind might not fare better with a somewhat less complete security, which could and would still have much better safeguards than exist in the present situation.

However we may picture for ourselves the final goal of a reasonably stable world peace, there are many more modest tasks to be performed in the meantime. First of all is the task of armaments limitation. The suggestion that this be accomplished by total unilateral disarmament would involve too great a political risk for the side that disarms for this to be a responsible act. Moreover total mutual disarmament can hardly be the first step. So the task takes the form of a long-drawn-out process of arms limitation, the distant goal of which can at best be conceived of as extensive disarmament. Arms limitation does not necessarily need to take the form of a disarmament treaty. It can, as the American scholar Thomas C. Schelling has shown, in many cases be more effective by a tacit agreement between the two great powers. The individual steps that are possible here are in general beyond the influence of the ordinary citizens of a second- or third-rank power such as the Federal Republic of Germany. An exception would perhaps be a project such as the establishment of a zone in central Europe that would be free of atomic weapons, as the Polish Foreign Minister proposed a number of years ago and has repeated on several occasions. In the Federal Republic this proposal has not received the serious consideration it deserves, but in consequence of the recent changes in the structure of NATO, such consideration is perhaps more nearly possible now than it was earlier. In any case it should not be wrecked by the remarkable interest of the West German government in having a weapon system with atomic capability. It would be difficult to regard this interest, like many other wishes for a voice in the use of atomic weapons, as anything else than the expression of a deviant need for a national status symbol, if it did not also involve the idea of something that could be traded in the negotiations for German unity. But the idea that it would be possible to achieve the reunification of Germany on Western terms by negotiations that would include the renunciation of weapons with atomic capability, to which we must hold fast for the time being, is only a part of a concept of a German unification policy that in the meantime has become outmoded and has proven impractical. A government that in the interest of a national will-o'-the-wisp of this sort would today reject participation in an atomic weapon free zone in central Europe would bear heavy responsibility for passing up a significant contribution to world peace. On the other hand, recent German suggestions for a renunciation of force could take more concrete form by even now taking the Polish suggestion into consideration, and the efforts to achieve an understanding with Germany's neighbors in the East would thereby be made considerably easier. Other demands advanced today for a German renunciation of an expensive delivery system for atomic weapons and for restricting the defense forces to purely defensive tasks could be combined with the concept of an atom-free zone in central Europe, which would then be the central feature of German efforts toward world peace.

In addition to the efforts toward limitation of weapons, actions that help in the prevention of war include the discovery and modification of psychological dispositions among the people which, under certain circumstances, could produce a willingness to go to war. The clarification of aggressive positions and projections, as well as efforts to decrease them, constitutes an area in which each citizen, regardless of social standing or role, can easily make a contribution to peace.

The projection onto the enemy of one's own repressed aggression, especially in a time of preparation for war, and increasingly during its course, can result in a progressive dehumanizing of the enemy, who is no longer seen as an individual but as a specimen of a hostile category of human beings. Fulbright characterized an American war report from Vietnam as describing the hunting down of an individual Vietcong not as the killing of a human being but as the destruction of something abstract and subhuman, that is, a "communist." Who can help being reminded of our own not-too-distant past in which the label of subhuman was intended to weaken or extinguish the feeling of human solidarity with Jews, Bolsheviks, and Poles.

The most effective defense against such clichés would certainly be the reduction of the aggression that produce them. In individual cases this can be done by showing genuine love for a child or an adult, thus overcoming his insecurity and anxiety. It can also come about through the recognition which society grants to an individual. Therefore the inner peace that exists in a society, the amount of righteousness and mutual recognition in relations between the groups in a society, has direct significance for the preservation of external peace. A society filled with extreme tensions is more likely to regard its opponents as devils and in this way restore a degree of solidarity within its own ranks.

In view of the many and varied sources of aggression in modern society, however, it is not enough merely to attack the causes of stereotyped characterizations, especially those of other peoples. As I have said, there are too many roots and causes of aggression for that to be sufficient. The dehumanizing cliché must be unmasked as the product of one's own aggressions and exposed to public contempt as something dishonorable. Stereotypes that other peoples have of us Germans are not to be answered by our clichés of them, and thereby given the status of established concepts. Rather, they should arouse dismay and sorrow, and they can be countered only with great patience. It is especially important to see even in the representative of a hostile ideology or the officials of a nation we regard as our enemy the individual human instead of the ideological cliché. And, though it should not really be necessary to add this, even the German police should not think of students primarily as rioters. To quote Fulbright once more: "Man's capacity for decent behavior seems to vary directly with his perception of others as individual humans with human motives and feelings, whereas his capacity for barbarous behavior seems to increase with his perception of an adversary in abstract terms." Everyone can help do away with dehumanizing stereotypes, which are especially dangeous when they take on ideological coloring, and the way to do this is to learn to think and to help others think of even our national or ideological enemies first of all as human beings with human anxieties, motives, and feelings. This could perhaps be the most significant contribution of Christians in all lands toward the prevention of war and toward progress on the road to a peaceful world for all mankind. The peace that God has given us through the death and resurrection of Jesus should enable us to become freer of our own insecurity and anxiety and the aggressions that they produce and to put aside the distorted pictures of members of other groups, other nations, and other world views, which hinder them and us from finding the way to mutual understanding.

The cause of preventing war would also be served if war were morally outlawed. Here theology has a special task. Since traditional theological ethics has generally affirmed the possibility of a just war, special care must be given to each new formulation of the Christian concept of peace at this point. Here it will be seen whether that concept can stand up against a political reality that is always characterized by tensions and conflicts, or whether through compromises in the course of world events it will become ineffective, or whether it will gloss over the actual situations of conflict in a fanciful manner and in this way become ineffectual.

First it must be conceded that the doctrine of the just war does not involve in any way a glorification of war itself, but instead is concerned to limit and humanize war. But anyone who is not prepared to let heroic language conceal the gruesome reality of technologically perfected mass murder, and anyone who will not be deceived by the Medusa face of war in the atomic age must still pose the question, in spite of such sober knowledge of the situation, whether in specific situations, such as defense against unprovoked aggression, war is not unavoidable and therefore justified.

To anticipate the answer, I do not believe that the thesis can be defended that while the concept of a just war was tenable in earlier ages, even by Christians, it is no longer tenable because of the development of atomic weapons. The unprecedented increase in the destructive power of nuclear weapons is not a sufficient basis for the alleged categorical difference. The death of a few in war, or even the death of a single individual, especially a civilian, cannot be deemed acceptable to a Christian in contrast to the killing of a large number. We are not to forget that the parables of Jesus ascribe infinite value to the life of each individual. The God of Jesus takes infinite interest in the one lost sheep and in each of "the least of these," as Jesus said, but it is easy to forget their plight. The quantity of killing is of course not simply a morally neutral concern, but even the killing of one person cannot be justified in Christian terms. The degree of horror which a modern war unleashes must help us realize that the idea of a "just war" is untenable, at least for a Christian. Otherwise it is difficult to judge the concept of just war as inapplicable in the atomic age merely because of the greater destructive power of nuclear weapons. There is, however, a more convincing argument for this position. This is the fact that in the present state of weapons technology the commitment of nuclear weapons by one of the great powers against the other would have as its consequence at least a corresponding degree of destruction for the attacker. Insofar as this situation excludes the possibility of victory in a nuclear war, the traditional concept of just war is in reality inapplicable. That concept demands, in addition to a just reason for war, a just goal, for which there is no room in the case of predictable mutual destruction, not to mention the equally necessary appropriateness of the means to be used. But this situation of a balance of terror could be altered at least temporarily by further progress in the technology of armaments, for example, by antimissile missiles; and if the inapplicability of the concept of just war rests only on the threat of mutual destruction, this basis could be so unstable that the possibility might arise that in a different political situation the validity of the concept might again become something that could be discussed. It seems to me that in any case the Christian "No" to a justification of war must have a deeper basis, and that a critical revision of the traditional concept of the just war must be undertaken; one cannot rest satisfied with the conviction that it is inapplicable in the atomic age, which means, strictly speaking, only in the present state of weapons technology.

The more far-reaching verdict must be that the concept of a just war is a fiction. There is no such thing as a just war and there probably never has been.

This verdict cannot be rejected as the expression of a fanatical pacifism. The rejection of war does not mean surrender to the illusion of a world without conflicts. Conflict and war are basically different categories, and it is one of the means by which war is made harmless to designate it as a mere conflict. In a conflict there is a clash of opposing interests that demand resolution. War, on the contrary, proceeds from the abandonment of hope in the possibility of a resolution and is directed toward the destruction of the opponent or at least of his ability to fight. There is thus no reason for regarding conflict and war as analogous. Further, the statement that there probably never has been such a thing as a just war does not mean that wars have always been avoidable. There can be just reasons for a country and its citizens to defend themselves by taking up arms against an unprovoked attack. Further, there can even be good grounds for anticipating an attack that is certain to come. But even a war that arises in such a manner is not a just war, not even for the side that is attacked or for the party that is driven to the desperate step of launching a preemptive strike. War remains an immeasurable and incalculable evil that through the hostility aroused by the will to mutual destruction drives those who wage it far beyond any just and perhaps unavoidable occasion that may have been there at its origin. The longer a war lasts the more gruesome it becomes. It is never possible for a belligerent, even one who has taken up the struggle for highly honorable reasons, to come out of the war as righteous as he entered it. It is fiction that a war that has once broken out can be kept within certain moral limits, when these seem to hinder the overriding goal of defeating the enemy. The drive to destroy represents the inner law of war, from which not even those can escape who have begun the struggle from honorable motives such as defense against an unprovoked attack, and therefore war cannot be just. If justice, in the sense of mutually respected ways of life, is closely connected with peace, then the concept of a just war is like that of wooden iron. It is possible to oppose the self-righteousness of the parties to a war only when the attribute of righteousness is denied to war absolutely and without exception. Such self-righteousness has usually contributed to a dulling of moral sensitivity toward reprehensible acts as soon as those acts seem to contribute to the reputedly just cause of defeating the enemy. The consciousness of having a just cause results in a complacency that cannot be permitted to any party to a war. Only so can the possible weight of moral pressure—no matter how modest it may be—be brought to bear on hastening the termination of hostilities.

In the present international political situation war is not completely avoidable. And that is true not only of wars of defense. As long as wars of aggression are outlawed morally and by international law, but there is no reliable and effective way of preventing military aggression, even the decision to wage a preventive war cannot be regarded as absolutely reprehensible in certain emergencies. But where this is the case we always find the hypocrisy of each side accusing the other of having attacked first.

Violent revolutions and civil wars will break out from time to time, as long as there are no other ways to change the government of the nations involved. A situation of international peace that perpetuated the existing relationships between the rulers and the ruled would leave no room for the search for a righteousness that would transform the status quo. But peace without righteousness brings only the tyrannical peace of the cemetery. Revolutions and civil war become unnecessary and avoidable where there are democratic institutions that make it possible to have a peaceful transfer of power. Such institutions, however, must not remain empty political forms that allow the existing power structure to continue undisturbed.

A peaceful world order that could be regarded as a foreshadowing of the future Lordship of God would have to include both the effective prevention of aggression and rules for the peaceful transfer of power in the individual nation-states. So long as such rules are not universally recognized, it is necessary to reckon with the encouragement of civil wars by one of the great powers and thus also with the intervention by the forces of the other great power. This can lead to a tragic situation like that in Hungary or Vietnam. The Hungarian insurrection and the Vietnam War were tragic in character, because in both cases a revolutionary movement, which in its origins was not the result of external interference, was regarded by one of the great powers as being due to such interference and was answered by military intervention and war.

Unfortunately it would be an illusion to expect that the moral pressure resulting from outlawing war would either prevent wars or bring them to a quick end. Such pressure can work only indirectly, first on the government of each person's own country and then on the international scene through world opinion, but in both cases only as one factor among many. But if we are going to accomplish as much as possible, Christians must join together to express their position publicly in the framework of a democratic society. Preparations should be made in the local parishes, so that the declarations of representative organizations on the national and international level are not left hanging in the air, as is largely the case today, but express in comprehensive manner the judgments formed within the churches. There must also be an attempt to join with non-Christian groups that are traveling the same road in search of peace in order to be able to join with them in a common stand.

Such protest activities are especially appropriate in situations like the Vietnam War, where one world power became involved as the result of intervention in a civil war. In limited wars where neither of the great powers is directly involved, a quick end to hostilities can be achieved because of a shared interest of the great powers in the preservation of world peace and through joint pressure on the belligerents; but if one of the great powers is directly engaged, this possibility does not exist. It is here that today the still-weak voice of moral protest constitutes one of the few counter influences. Thus Christians bear a special responsibility in the struggle for peace, especially in relationships with a power that appeals to the concept of freedom and thus to its Christian heritage for justification of its political actions.

It is regrettable that the possibility for public protest against such a war really exists only in the Western democracies, while in countries with other forms of government Christians must exercise their political responsibility within much narrower bounds. Since it is the nature of democratic protests that they are primarily addressed to one's own government or to powers allied with one's own country, with which the protesters would otherwise like to identify, the false impression is easily given that such criticism is directed exclusively and one-sidedly to the Western governments. Yet it is obvious that declarations directed to regimes whose citizens have no possibility of exercising such criticism do not fulfill the function of a democratic critique, but are dismissed as the echo of the official governmental policies of the West and thus have no effect except perhaps that of deepening the ideological differences between East and West. We could wish that these special conditions of the perception of political responsibility on the part of Christians would be recognized by the governments involved and not misinterpreted with inappropriate indignation as actions of left-wing Protestants or intellectuals. Criticism is expression of solidarity with one's own democratic government, not the breach of that solidarity. We also ought to recognize that by the exercise of such activities of political self-criticism the citizen is documenting his positive participation in the democratic life of his society. This is especially true for Christians, who are thus reaffirming in the name of God's future kingdom their freedom in respect to present reality.

Thus far a number of hints have been given as to the type of world peace which Christians—insofar as my judgment is correct—can regard as the harbinger of God's future reign. First it is characterized by a system of world peace which we are to strive to establish, and which must have a sufficient degree of independence and authority over the nations to effectively prevent aggression, so that preventive wars would be unnecessary. We Christians regard the relatively peaceful condition of the world today, as far as it extends, as something which we gratefully accept as the grace of God and as a sign of his kingdom of peace. This present peace often seems like a miracle, but it is not enough simply to accept the miracle. Certainly we must not become so accustomed to it that we take it for granted. Humans should not be passive recipients of God's actions. It is our destiny to participate responsibly in God's Lordship over the world. In terms of the issues we are dealing with here, his Lordship can find its universal, although provisional, expression in a world order characterized by peace. That is the first thing.

Second, this world order must leave room for changes in political relationships, room for the search for greater righteousness, in the internal life of a nation and in the relations of the nations to one another. Both of these could scarcely be achieved through a world government to which the great powers would have to cede so much military power that it would be stronger than either of them. No one should assume that the opposing great powers would agree to such an extensive surrender of sovereignty. The more likely way to peace seems to be that of patient effort for cooperation between the great powers, which, in spite of all setbacks, still in general is moving forward. This can be embodied in treaties only in exceptional cases or after the fact. Such increasing cooperation, however, must move beyond the military sphere and include an understanding about the rules that should cover changes in the relationship between the governed and those who govern so that civil wars and intervention in internal affairs would be unnecessary.

Along such lines a pluralistic world society is conceivable that would develop through increasing commonality of interests and responsibilities. It is also certain that as a secondary matter it would become institutionalized, but that can hardly be the starting point. This must by no means take the form of a centralized authority exercised by a world government whose power would completely exclude any misuse of power by the individual states. It would be preferable to work out an international equivalent of the democratic institutions that provide for a balance of interests. Christians should not lose sight of the fact that the pluralism of mutually limiting forces can be the human equivalent of the unity of God's Lordship, while the unlimited power of a single authority all too easily takes on the features of the Antichrist. Only the Lordship of God is both universal and humane. The only human who as an individual symbolized the Lordship of God for mankind did so, not through the exercise of political power, but through the weakness of a criminal's death.

Does peace really exist among us? Where does the universal peace of God invade the political situation of our world? If it does so anywhere, it is in the processes of mutual recognition and cooperation between such different partners on a basis of equality in their cooperation for a truly human existence for all, beyond the distinctions of conflicting special interests and ideologies. The task has been placed in our hands of seeing that the biblical picture of the opposite of the peace of God, the catastrophe of apocalyptic destruction, does not transform our earth into a lifeless, cratered landscape.

The basic principle of mutual recognition and cooperation between different partners must not be limited to international relationships. There must be mutual recognition of differing life-styles and views as alternative ways of moving toward the realization of our common humanity, both in the social structures of our nations and within the life of our families. Wherever the limits of one's own position—and thus the right of others to lead their own lives—is recognized, there honor is given to God, who alone is unlimited in his truth and justice. And that will also be the peace of God, which has its origin in the cross of Christ.

9

THE FUTURE
AND THE UNITY OF MANKIND

As is the case with other topics, there is in discussions of the future no general agreement in the use of terminology, no common language. Differing judgments about issues often depend on hidden relationships to differing linguistic usage. This is no less the case for theologians than in the wider context of intellectual discussions. At times one may complain that the problem is even more acute among theologians, so that at least in this respect theology can feel that it stands on heights not always attained by other disciplines. The lack of a common language is, however, not so lamentable a matter as it may seem to some. It makes possible the emergence of new points of view that otherwise might be excluded from discussion. In addition, it provides a stimulus to overcome differences of language by a deeper penetration into the issues themselves, and thus arouses a concern to achieve a more profound understanding. The differences of interpretation and of the use of language, if they are not entirely trivial, can help us discover a common point of reference, at the very least a starting point, from which the subject is developed in opposing directions.

I

In a similar manner, it seems to me, it also ought to be possible to assume a common point of reference for both theological discussions of the future and secular futurology.

When theologians speak of the future, characteristically they usually stress the newness of that which lies in the future. This feature might have central significance for theological conceptions that are otherwise quite distinct. The reason for this is found in the context of the eschatological consciousness. The stress on what is new in the existential moment and also in the otherness of God and of his revelation in contrast to all that is human and worldly may be traced back to the Christian eschatological consciousness and the rediscovery of eschatology in the years since the beginning of this century. This eschatological theme constitutes the common point of reference of the differing theological interpretations of the future.

In one way or another the phenomenon of newness is significant for everything that is said concerning the future. Yet in the perspectives that are dominant for secular futurologists the future is anticipated by extrapolating from present tendencies, or models are developed that are intended to represent trends of that sort. Theology, on the other hand, deals with a future that confronts the present world and all its developmental tendencies and even stands in opposition to it. This understanding of the future is especially characteristic for the so-called theology of hope and other theological conceptions that have been developed in Europe on the basis of the exegetical rediscovery of early Christian eschatology.[1] But it is less characteristic of the work of Teilhard de Chardin. To be sure, even Teilhard could stress the priority of the Omega point over the process of evolution, but on the other hand he conceived of this process in terms of a teleological tendency (orthogenesis) at its beginnings, so that the future of the Omega point is seen as an extrapolation from this process.[2] It is even less appropriate to characterize the lines of thought in Whitehead's philosophy by the concept of a future that confronts the present and does not merely extend it. Even here, however, the idea that God provides each new event with its own "subjective aim" makes it possible to give a Christian interpretation to the present in the perspective of its eschatological future,[3] at least to the same degree as is true of Bultmann's concept of the future nature of Christian existence. The interpretation of the newness of events as the expression of a subjective aim that God has bestowed on each of them can be understood as the future nature, not only of human existence, but of all events.

For Christian theology the concept of God is intimately connected with the contingent nature of new occurrences and thus with the future. This finds expression in the doctrine of the incarnation as well as in the concept of promise and of the hope to which the promise gives rise. But God's future, which is announced in that promise, is not simply a contrast to the existing structures of the world. One of the reasons lies in the concept of promise itself, because promise expresses a positive relationship of the announced future to the present reality. In contrast to threats of judgment and destruction, promises have a positive relationship to the fundamental interests of the existential situation. This corresponds to the dynamic of divine love, which does not simply reject the present reality of the created world but affirms it in its proper essence, although its intention may be to transform it into a form truer to its real destiny. This positive relationship to both present and past reality, in spite of all criticism of it, was established once for all by the incarnation of God in Jesus Christ. Belief in the incarnation means that the future will not simply destroy the past and the present. God's future is rather seen in many respects as an extrapolation of the story and as the proclamation of Jesus of Nazareth, and this story in turn was based on and has as its content the breaking through of the future of God into present reality.

All this indicates that futurological extrapolation of trends observed in the present and theological confrontation between the present and God's future are not mutually exclusive. It is especially the case that the models which futurologists have developed to combat the threat to human life which may be anticipated from current tendencies can correspond in a significant way to theological anticipations of the future of mankind and the world in the sense of promise and hope. The greatest difference between them seems to be that extrapolations are most reliable in respect to the immediate or to the near future, while theology is primarily concerned with the ultimate destiny of human beings and the world. Nevertheless, in view of the rapidly increasing rate of change in the modern world, futurology is today concerned with the distant future, which a theologian might characterize as the middle distant future, while on the other hand theology, which has the final future of God as its theme, relates it to contemporary conditions in order to provide a stimulus for finding solutions for the needs of the present day and of the immediate future.

II

The theological assumption that the future is not simply an extrapolation from and a continuation of past and present but a reality in its own right is based on the concept of God. Even if God is understood, not as the power of the future itself, but more in the sense of traditional concepts as an eternal being, it is still a part of the doctrine of creation that God continuously brings forth new creations and thus confronts each present time with a future that is different from it. And even in a more traditional view, which thinks of God without limitations as infinite being existing in the here and now, God is not only the creator but also the future of mankind and the world. All Christian theology agrees that the whole creation is destined to participate in the glory of God and by this participation to become glorified itself.

The idea of God as the future of the world gives expression in a particularly decisive manner to the theological understanding of the future as an independent reality that confronts the present. At the same time it contains a point of contact with the extrapolated future of futurology, and it is to this issue that the following discussion is devoted.

The God who confronts the present world with its future, and who is himself the final future of mankind, is one God. If, however, the one God is the final future of mankind, then the further development of humanity must tend in the direction of an increasing unity of the human race. Teilhard de Chardin's main theme, the concept of the unity of creation, is then seen as a necessary implication of the unity of God as soon as this one God is no longer thought of only as the origin of his creation, but also as the goal of its final destiny and consummation. This assumes that his creative activity is not separated from his creatures but united to them by the purgatory of his judgment, which will bring about the reconciliation and unification of all of creation. At this point Teilhard's vision is very close to the early Christian expectation of the coming Kingdom of God, and especially to the interpretation of this expectation with its awareness that the reality of the creator himself is inseparably bound up with the coming of his kingdom.

From this point of view the power of reconciliation is not something supplementary that was to be added on to God's creative reality as an action of a totally different nature. Unconditioned, creative, and reconciling love is characteristic of the work of the creator himself, and through it the process of evolution was drawn more and more deeply into the center of the creative force, in spite of all the tendencies of God's creatures to self-isolation, self-preservation, indolence, and aggression. In this sense human evolution is a process of reconciliation that overcomes the horrors of human history and is increasingly closer to the heart of God than were the earlier stages in the development of life. But here Christian faith is also concerned with the heart of the power that created all things.

To a large extent this approach is common to Teilhard de Chardin and the theologies that are concerned with the eschatological future. It is more difficult to decide whether there is at this point also a correspondence to the process philosophy of the school of Whitehead. To be sure, also in Whitehead's perspective God is the source of unity in that he provides each event with its subjective aim, which it then achieves when it subjectively integrates its world. Would it not be possible to interpret this subjective integration of the current world by each new event as a step of participation in God's act of creation in the sense of Teilhard's creative unification? The only difficulty is that in Whitehead's own thought creativity is separated from the concept of God. As a consequence it seems that Whitehead's God can scarcely be understood as creator of the world in the precise sense of creation out of nothing, but it also seems, and this might be even more serious, that this results in an unlimited pluralism, an unlimited, continuing series of events, each of which constitutes a subjective unit but does not converge with all the others in a lineal unity of all reality. At this important point it may be possible—as John Cobb has attempted—to develop further in a Christian sense Whitehead's concept of God by subordinating the principle of creativity to God as the supreme entity.[4] It is in any case difficult to make a correction of this sort without there being far-reaching consequences for the network of concepts in Whitehead's philosophical system, especially since God, if we accept Cobb's correction, must be understood as the originator of contingent existence and not as simply providing each event with a formal idea of itself. But whatever consequences might result from subordinating the principle of creativity to the creative activity of God, Teilhard's concept of a convergence of the process of evolution toward a final unity through participation in the one God no longer needs to be excluded in principle from the perspective of a process theology inspired by Whitehead. On the contrary, if love constitutes the ultimate motif of God's creative activity, and when it is the nature of love that the one who loves discloses himself to the beloved (at least to the extent that that would best serve the interests of the beloved), then the completion of the process of evolution in a convergence in which the creatures would take part in the unity of the creator himself involves the very essence of the act of creation as such. This does not mean that the creature has any claim on God; rather, it is contained in the inner logic of the creative love of God himself.

III

The foregoing discussion has shown with increasing clarity that the prospect of a unified humanity is the point of contact, the intersection of divine reality with the extrapolated tendencies of human history and even the total evolution of organic life.

In the Christian tradition the concept of a point at which divine and human reality intersect was regarded as the special privilege of the person of Jesus Christ. And in fact Jesus Christ was not only the prophet of the coming kingdom but also its Messiah and the pioneer and head of a new humanity. His Messianic function did not however allow him to hold fast to his nearness to God as a privilege, but it was expressed in his enabling others to participate in the Kingdom of God. That means working for justice and peace among all mankind. The Kingdom of God, the coming of which Jesus proclaimed and which became present reality for his hearers in and through that proclamation, is identical with the ultimate reality of God himself and connected with the reconciliation of all humans in a society of peace and justice, which the prophets of the Old Testament proclaimed in the midst of the social and political reality of their own time. Belief in a loving God can be justified only through the future of God, when his love reaches its fulfillment through the reconciliation that puts an end to all the suffering and error of his creatures.

It is obvious that this concept of the Kingdom of God far excels anything that could be accomplished by human effort. But in spite of its transcendent nature, the concept of the Kingdom of God constitutes the criterion by which the actual accomplishments of social and political efforts and changes must be measured. There is a correspondence between the future of the Kingdom and the forces that seem to be blindly at work in the process of human history, in spite of all the shortcomings and distortions of which this history is full. Even the social and political movement toward the unity of humanity remains quite ambivalent. It is always the scene of a struggle for power. And yet its correspondence to the universal unity of the coming Kingdom of God is substantiated by the fact that human history, with all its perversion, remains the creation of God, toward whose kingdom it is moving.

For Teilhard de Chardin the phenomenon of a converging drift in the evolution of the human race, and especially in the modern phase of human history, was of the greatest significance. While in the evolution of life we can generally observe diverging tendencies in the formation of an amazing multiplicity of species and of innumerable individuals, there is at the level of the human race an opposite tendency, a drift toward unity. The decisive factor in this transition in the evolutionary process is, in Teilhard's eyes, the human capability of reflective thought. Unfortunately Teilhard did not define his concept of human reflection more precisely. Still it is clear that he regarded reflection as involving the human capability to form general concepts, and this capability made possible the convergence of human history through the uniting of individuals. The hint that humans are social beings to the degree in which they are reflecting beings requires more careful elaboration than Teilhard gave to it. But it does involve a decisive insight because the mutual relationship of the individual and society is the painful point at which all human problems come to a focus, especially those problems which bear on the future of humanity. Teilhard's scanty comments on the role of human reflection can be supplemented by the observation that the human capacity to grasp general concepts is related to the fact that humans do not possess the unity of their existence within themselves and are therefore constantly on the search for a unity that transcends the individual, and in which the individual can feel a sense of belonging. George

Herbert Mead's contention that even the identity of the individual is a fact of social life may illustrate this relationship. Because a human being does not find any ultimate unity within himself, the unity of society is in a quite specific manner constitutive of the identity of the individual person, although the individual is searching for the universal unity that transcends all existing social unity and brings it into question.

In connection with the reflective nature of human existence, the constant increase in population (and in modern times the acceleration of that increase) has specific meaning for the evolution of the human race. The growth in population brought with it the expansion of humanity over the whole face of the earth. In reality this took the form of the economic and political expansion of certain societies and led to conflicts and wars. Because of the development and application of science and technology this expansion has in modern times entered a period of acceleration that reached a critical height with atomic technology. Teilhard was apparently correct in his assumption that this process resulted in increasing pressure for the socialization of humanity on a world scale. The population growth that resulted from modern medicine and improved communication and trade following the industrial revolution constituted only the opening phase of the acceleration of this process in the modern phase of human history. With the development of nuclear weapons, military technology reached a point that made the search for peace urgent, at least between the great powers. It has been claimed that in the long run this also includes the urgency of developing some form of world government.[5] However that may be, Alvin Toffler was correct in saying that already today "the network of social ties is so tightly woven that the consequences of contemporary events radiate instantaneously around the world."[6] The shocks that the Vietnam War sent around the world are a ready illustration of the truth of this observation.

IV

Teilhard de Chardin regarded the trend toward convergence in modern history with a feeling of confidence. He did recognize, however, some of the negative aspects of the increasing density of population, and he was aware of the tendency to increasing aggressiveness, to intensified nervous demands, and to the spread of neuroses. Still he viewed these problems as only temporary. The increased density of population would lead, he felt, to the formation of groups of individuals and to the organization of their life together on a new level of development, with the result that interpersonal tensions would abate. This might be a possible solution to the problems of the present historical situation, but such a solution is by no means certain and the dangers involved must not be ignored or underestimated. Teilhard himself was aware of the possibility of perverting the modern convergence toward unity by the manipulation and standardization of the masses, which would lead to an anthill of an almighty collective state instead of the ideal of the universal brotherhood of man. But Teilhard regarded these alarming tendencies as merely passing deviations from the course of evolution. He underestimated the depths of alienation in the development of society that would lead to the perfect manipulation which is possible in a "megamachine society," as Erich Fromm[7] called it.

On the one hand it is surely true that there will be no future for human beings without association with all other human beings. Teilhard's harsh verdict on the "heresy" of individualism contains a sizable element of truth. This judgment is applicable to more than the tendency to isolate oneself by retreating into private life, in the sense of traditional middle-class individualism. It is especially applicable to certain romanticized reactions against the bureaucratic perfection of the "system" of society, views that like to style themselves as radical or revolutionary, but which are in reality only a powerless protest against the restrictions that modern society imposes on the life of the individual. Such romantic reactions are fond of appealing to the right of the individual to develop all his natural gifts and to satisfy all his individual needs and wishes. Such tendencies in the subculture and also in the psychological and pedagogical thought of our time are colorful enough to have an appeal, and they often merit at least our sympathy. But in the final analysis they are romantic, because the increasing density of population and the increasing diversity of the possibilities, and thus the decisions, which the individual has to confront, demand the opposite of such romantic visions, that is, a greater degree of discipline, of mutual respect and consideration among individuals. The restrictions on our life together mean that space for unlimited arbitrariness even in the sanctuary of private life, which in the future must continue to provide healing for the harshness of life in society, must be restricted even more in the interests of our fellow humans.

The pressure toward increased conformity is enormous in both social life and politics. But at the same time, the tensions between the individual and society continue to exist. The broad interests of a society can be articulated only by certain individuals and must be safeguarded by their actions. For this reason the public interest is again and again abused by individuals who have been entrusted with safeguarding it, but who use it to serve their own goals and special interests. In this way the anonymous structures of social organization serve to conceal the continued domination of some persons by others. And this does not hold true only for the capitalistic societies of the Western world; it is true also of the power structures in noncapitalist lands. The exploitation of the common interest by individuals who have been charged with protecting it is so deeply entrenched in the present conditions of human existence that for the foreseeable future any attempt to put a final end to alienation will be shipwrecked on those conditions. Anyone who does not take this situation into account will inevitably fall victim to ideological illusions.

These last observations help to strengthen my basic contention that the individual must remain the goal and the standard of the systems of society. Naturally this contention can easily be misused or misunderstood as carte blanche for arbitrary individualism. Its justification consists primarily in the fact that only so can the abuse of political or economic power be prevented, assuming that the latter is not itself declared to be a private matter. Beyond this function of my basic position it also includes the recognition of the fact that every conceivable improvement of the conditions of human life must improve the situation of individuals, since "mankind" exists only in the form of individual humans. Of course the destiny of the individual points beyond this isolated existence, but any unity beyond the individual that makes it possible to lead a reflective existence can be attained only through the inspiration of personal freedom. Therefore, the measure by which the forms of life in society are judged must continue to be, not individual caprice, but the free person. What is it that distinguishes responsible persons, who are to be respected and encouraged, from arbitrary individuals on whom limits must be placed whenever they violate the social or natural conditions of the life of other humans? The question of such criteria proves finally to be a religious question, because the distinction between responsible freedom and undiscriminating recklessness depends on the answer given to the question, "In what does our human destiny consist?"

V

The ambiguities in the movement of convergence toward the unity of humanity, which is characteristic of the present period of human history, have become clearer in the course of this discussion. They grow out of the tensions between the individual and the social destiny of humanity. On the one hand, individuals do not yet possess within them in their innermost being the meaning of their existence. In order to come to oneself it is necessary to have a unity that lies beyond self, and this is present in concrete form in the group or the society to which the individual belongs. On the other hand, society should take the individual as its standard, because otherwise there will inevitably be oppression of individuals in the name of the interests of the total society, or even in the name of humanity, both of which are in reality represented by other individuals and their judgments. This is the involved situation, which to all appearances permits no simple elimination of alienation. In addition to the alienation resulting from the conscious official actions that deny the individual the right to his own free opinion, there is the opposite alienation of an individualistic private sphere that denies to the individual the consciousness of a unity of truth beyond his own arbitrary decisions and yet communicates to the individual the feeling of being ruled by others who enrich themselves through exploiting his fundamental human needs.

A final resolution of the antagonism between the individual and society clearly remains an eschatological ideal. It is improbable that such a resolution would be attained under the current conditions of human history. It would be possible only if humans were by nature good in the sense that they worked for their individual satisfaction only within the framework of what is best for all and did not use what is best for all as the means of satisfying their own interests. But humans are not good in this sense, and therefore the antagonism between individuals and society, or that among individuals, cannot be finally eliminated under the current conditions of our lives or under any similar conditions. The final elimination of all alienation would mean the achievement of our human destiny, that of the individual as well as that of society, and it would require that there be a place in that complete society for all individuals. This is just what is meant by the eschatological symbolism of the Jewish and Christian tradition. It finds expression in the uniting of the Kingdom of God and the resurrection of the dead. The expectation of the Kingdom of God includes the conviction that only when God alone reigns and no human any longer has political power over other humans, will the lordship of humans over other humans and the inevitable injustice that accompanies this will come to an end. The alternative to the rule of humans over other humans is therefore not self-government, because those who rule or who take part in providing for the common good always constitute a small minority. The true alternative to the rule of some humans over others is the Lordship of God. It alone can eliminate human rule and bring about a society in which humans no longer rule over their fellow humans, thus achieving the social destiny of mankind.

The second condition mentioned above for a social realization of human destiny was that all individuals participate in it. This participation should include the specification that each individual should be allowed to take part to the extent to which he or she is qualified to do so. That can naturally be accomplished only when all human individuals are present. A resurrection of the dead is necessary if all individuals of all times are to find their appropriate role in the perfect society of the Kingdom of God. Only with this provision can it be said that the destiny of mankind, and mankind means the full number of all its individuals, has been fulfilled. If the social and the individual destinies of humans are interrelated, so that they can only be realized together, then it is necessary to have the total number of all human individuals present for human social destiny to be realized. It is then not enough to hope that a later generation in a more or less distant future will achieve a perfect society. That would only mean that the present generation had sacrificed the happiness that should have been its lot for the sake of a future generation—a sacrifice that is customarily demanded without the one who is being sacrificed having given his free consent. By contrast, the symbolic language of the Jewish-Christian eschatological expectation sets precise conditions for the final accomplishment of human destiny in a truly human society.

VI

What kind of future is it to which the symbolic language of Jewish-Christian apocalyptic points? There can be no doubt that the eschatological future is understood as a true future, in the sense that it is not yet present but is still to come. In addition, the eschatological future has often been understood as an event in a line of other events in the ongoing world process and in human history. But it is here that questions arise. A general resurrection of the dead would clearly be an event to which no other event could be compared. How could we then view it as a member of this line of events which is composed of events of quite ordinary nature? If in some sense a general resurrection of the dead follows after other events, then we should assume that the chronological sequence itself is different in kind from that in series consisting entirely of ordinary events. This would lead us to think of a distortion of the usual form of chronological sequence in analogy to the curvature of space according to the theory of relativity.

Our doubts concerning the transition from ordinary historical events to those events to which the eschatological symbols of the Christian tradition refer grow greater when we read in the Jewish apocalyptic writings that the events which are to be revealed in the end time are already present in heaven. This way of thinking is found also in the New Testament, especially in the Gospel of John, where it says that the future judgment is already taking place now in the encounter with Jesus Christ, and that those who believe in his words already are participating in eternal life. The letter to the Colossians says similarly that Christians who have been baptized not only are united with the death of Christ and thereby have received the hope of their future resurrection, as Paul had taught; indeed, they already participate in the new life of the resurrection, even though this is hidden with God. And is it not strikingly similar to this way of thinking when it is said of Christ that even now, exalted but concealed with God, he reigns in heaven over the powers that rule this world? The messianic kingdom of the future is already present in heaven. And for the Gospel of Mark, Jesus was in a mysterious sense already during his earthly career the Messiah and the Son of Man. All this means that the eschatological future is in a certain sense already present, concealed, to be sure, in the divine secret, where the real meaning of the concept of heaven consists in something beyond the spatial picture of a divine region above the stars. The mode of thinking that recurs in all these concepts is applied even to God himself. His kingdom, and therefore the public exercise of his power, is still in the eschatological future, and yet God rules the world even now from the concealment of heaven.

The eschatological future is identical with the eternal being of things, just as the future of the Kingdom of God is identical with his eternal reality and power. Is such a future then not a true future? Indeed, the eschatological future is truly future, because the true nature of the things has not yet appeared. It is not yet perfect, and yet it involves the essence of things past and present, and thus that which really constitutes their being. It must therefore itself be in relationship to what is past or present. We must revise the traditional ways of understanding being and eternity in relationship to time. The being of things must not be understood in a timeless manner; it is dependent on the process of time, and only through the outcome of that process will it be determined whether it involves the identity of things that have long since disappeared. Similarly eternity—as the sphere of the structures of being—should not be thought of as timeless, but must be understood as being constituted by the historical process and especially by its outcome. On the other hand, time is not to be thought of as simply the sequence of isolated moments, but as a sequence of events that contribute to the identity (or to the essence) of things.

While Teilhard did not concern himself with such questions, I am aware that Whiteheadians must consider such assertions odd. Nevertheless I cannot regard a series of truly only momentary events[8] as anything but an abstract quantification of actual events; and a quantitative model of an event, must, remarkably enough, be supplemented by the assumption of a Platonic sphere of essences which are mere possibilities and which, in order to be realized, must enter into a process conceived of in abstract quantitative terms.[9] Yet in this process something arises, and this something is neither a mere aggregate of momentary events nor a mere possibility. It develops and has continuity, not only as an object, but also in itself. This is nothing else than what is called the substance or the essence of things. I agree with the process philosophers that the traditional concept of substance is problematic, because it is separated from existence and development in time. But I am not at all convinced that it is possible to dispense altogether. with the concept of essence. Thus if we bring together being and time, essence and existence in time, we become involved in the paradoxes of present and future to which I have already alluded. Then it is the ultimate future that will have to make the final decision as to what the essence of things is. That future then becomes the substance of the things about which it decides; it cannot be merely something external to them. On the other hand, it is not simply identical with the essence that is determined by it. That brings us back to the question of what kind of future the eschatological hope envisions. The answer can now be given. It involves the future of the essence of humanity, the achieving of human destiny. In other words, the eschatological hope anticipated the effect which unknown future events will have on the essence of mankind, both that of individuals and that of humanity as a whole. The eschatological hope rests on anticipation just as much as does every assumption about the nature of a phenomenon. It does distinguish explicitly between the present situation of humanity and our future destiny, but as is true of every anticipation, the eschatological hope leaves open the question of what specific events the anticipated future will bring.

The combination of future and eternity, which, as it developed in the Jewish-Christian eschatology, opens up the possibility of anticipating ultimate truth, is of particular significance for human self-understanding. Hope for humanity is never found exclusively in progress as such; the decisive question is where the progress is progressing to. People hope that they will attain a positive goal and that once attained it will not be lost again. Hope desires permanence. The measure of true progress is that it should not consist of continual and empty change. The fascination of progress depends on the degree to which its goals reflect eternity. Progress then not only approaches the goal, but while still under way it participates in it, because the future essence already penetrates into the present. The future essence, which contains the true destiny of present reality, participates in eternity and therefore constitutes the depths of reality, the secret of what is present. It is only because the future essence is already present in a hidden manner that it can be anticipated and can even now draw our personal life into its identity, even though the course that our life is taking still remains open. A future without eternity dwindles away in meaningless change, and if humanity is doomed to such a future empty of any essence, we are doomed to suffer future shock, because meaningless change threatens our personal identity. The accelerated change of styles, the masses of new data that continue to appear and to which we must relate, and the increasing complexity of the human social environment in the present and the foreseeable future—phenomena which Toffler has described so impressively—increase the danger of future shock and increase for more and more persons the difficulty of establishing a personal identity during their lifetime. On the other hand, only a strong personal identity can cope with the accelerating merry-go-round of change, the increasing pressure to buy new products, and the great number of possible choices in our society. I agree with Erich Fromm's view that a mere ability to conform is not enough to enable us to cope with this situation. Conformity robs a person of human dignity by making him or her an alienated, though still possibly useful, element in the "megamachine society." In order to preserve the human character of both private and public life, it is essential to have one's own personal identity. Identity, however, is possible only through anticipation of eternity. This is what Fromm meant when he called for "frames of orientation and devotion,"[10] which, in his opinion, are among the indispensable conditions of human existence. They provide individuals with a framework in which they can become oriented to themselves and to their world, with its unceasing changes, and they point individuals to the foundations of their human destiny. In the midst of the accelerating change and the resulting increase in the variety of new things and new possibilities, there is also increasing need for such "frames of orientation and devotion," so that we may establish zones of stability in the stream of life, where we will be able to withstand future shock.

VII

In stressing the human need for centers of orientation and commitment, we are posing the religious question. No individual can establish a personal identity by conforming to the changing styles of society, because society is made up of individuals, all of whom are equally fallible. In earlier periods of history, when the social order was still regarded as a copy of the eternal order of reality, it was easier than it is today to accept the standards of society in good conscience as the eternal truth itself. In a period of rapid and constantly accelerating social change, that is no longer possible. Even in those earlier historical periods the social order stood in need of a religious base. As Eric Voegelin[11] has contended, individual loyalty toward the social order can be based only on the assumption that the principles and symbolic institutions of a society represent the true nature of all reality. It is in this way that throughout history religion has repeatedly overcome the antagonism between the individual and the social order. Even the models of social order that are dominant today have in this general sense a religious basis. The models for a socialist society rest on the assumption that socialism represents the truth of human destiny, at least for the present period of history. The political principles of the Western democracies similarly rest on the assumption that they involve basic conditions of human dignity. But the principles of human freedom and equality are not self-evident, nor do they actually determine in an unmodified manner the structures of the social life in the societies of the West. They are not self-evident, because viewed empirically individuals are by no means equal. We are struck by the natural inequality of human beings, and at least the majority of individuals are not absolutely free. There is in any case a scale of degrees of freedom and equality. It is well known that Karl Marx's criticism of Western democracy was that these two principles are limited in the degree to which they determine the actual structure of social life. In middle-class democracy there is only a formal equality and a formal freedom, both of which conceal the existing inequality of the bases of life and thus of the necessary means for making use of freedom. The objection might be raised that such a formal freedom is still much better than none at all, and in reality this is the basis of the continuing superiority of the liberal democracies. But it is no very convincing justification for regarding them as preferable, and it is no ground for any great confidence in their chances for survival in view of the possibility of a liberalization of life in socialistic societies, which might well finally rob the middle-class democracies of the West of their fascination as a force for political development.

The greatest weakness of the democratic societies of the West remains, in the unanimous verdict of an increasing number of observers, the fact that the unity of society primarily depends on economic interests that constitute the common denominator for all individuals both in the processes of production and in the consumer sphere. Almost everything else is reduced to a private matter and thus abandoned to the laws of the marketplace, which determine the production and consumption of cultural goods, just as they do that of goods to satisfy private needs and desires. The cult of private life is only the reverse side of the tendentious limiting of the objective basis of our society to economic interests. But the aspiration for meaning in human life, which unites the individual with the rest of mankind, cannot be reduced either to economic interests or to private caprice. A large part of the unrest that has settled over so many citizens of the Western countries who are sensitive to the conditions for achieving human development, and consequently the unanticipated degree of fascination exerted by the quasi-religious character of the institutions of socialist societies, might be best explained in these terms.

The conclusion which I personally draw from all this is that the Western societies stand in desperate need of renewal and revision of their religious heritage, where the roots of their modern beginnings are found. The problem of the unity of a society is ultimately a religious problem, because the religious life expresses the consciousness of the future destiny of humanity, which can transcend the antagonism between the individual and society. Therefore religious issues cannot permanently be allowed to remain an exclusively private concern. The fact that in modern political constitutions religion has been made a private matter was surely necessary in view of the dogmatic intolerance that led to the religious wars at the beginning of the modern era. Sectarian intolerance had destroyed the peace of society, and thus the Christian religion could no longer constitute the basis of the unity of society. Even in the future, Christianity cannot again represent the spiritual unity of a society as long as it does not overcome the sectarian conflicts of its past. In addition, Christianity cannot overcome the problems of its own antagonistic traditions without considering the general problem of pluralism in religious thought and life—a problem closely connected with the provisional nature of all religious experience and certainty, in contrast to the ultimate truth about God and mankind, truth

that is not yet available to us but still belongs to the future, even
though this future has already been anticipated in Jesus Christ.
Such reflections on the provisional nature of our religious
consciousness can contribute to reconciliation among the
mutually antagonistic denominational traditions in Christianity; they can also enable Christians to become aware of the truth
of other religious traditions and perspectives. On the other
hand, this type of legitimation of the plurality of religious
experiences and religious thought within Christianity and even
beyond its bounds signifies a new and distinctively unified type
of religious thought. It would seem that this could prove
increasingly important for the future of society and for the
developing unity of humanity, if the religious or quasi-religious
bases of social life do not revert to a strongly authoritarian and
intolerant form. If we are to avoid this danger, and if pluralism is
to be strengthened in the forms of religious expression and
thought, without abandoning the unity of truth, then we must
make it clear that the new form of religious consciousness that
today is emerging out of innumerable ecumenical encounters
and dialogues is no longer a purely private concern.

Today there is a widespread feeling of disillusionment over
the ecumenical movement, and there are certainly many
reasons why this should be. But we should not overlook the fact
that the ecumenical movement could develop into the most
far-reaching contribution of present-day Christianity to the
political future of humanity and especially to that of the
Western world. This expectation is not primarily based on the
statements of the World Council of Churches on the problems
of social and political life. It would be a mistake to try to find the
significance of ecumenical activities principally in this realm of
social ethics. The relevance of the comments of ecumenical
organizations and representatives on social and political
problems depends ultimately on their religious competence in
the narrower sense. It is not proclamations about social ethics
but theological dialogue and religious reconciliation, which, if
they reach their goal, will have truly revolutionary conse-

quences for social and political life, because the religious problem is directly involved with the social and political unity of society. Anyone who is not already doing so should devote his efforts to the ecumenical unity of Christendom, because this involves, as does nothing else, the long-range aspects of the political responsibility of the Christian faith. Ecumenical dialogue is the point at which the eschatological destiny and future of mankind coincides most obviously with the tendencies of mankind to develop toward an increasing unity.

NOTES

1. SOCIETY AND THE CHRISTIAN FAITH

This essay was first published in *Christlicher Glaube und Gesellschaft,* ed. Ulrich Hommes, Düsseldorf, 1974.

2. ON THE THEOLOGY OF LAW

This essay was first published in *Zeitschrift für Evangelische Ethik* 7 (1963), pp. 1-23.

1. The following discussion, which is appearing simultaneously in the *Deutsche Richterzeitung,* was first presented as a lecture on June 17, 1962, before a meeting of the Evangelical Academy of Berlin. It was given in an earlier form in October 1959 at a working session of the Foundation for Studies in Bad Liebenzell. What was Part II in that version had been presented in condensed form in my radio talk "Justice Through Love," in the series "What Is Man?" (Göttingen, 1962, pp. 67-76; E.T. *What Is Man?* Fortress Press, 1970, pp. 96-109) and has been extensively revised in the new version. In the meantime, J. Moltmann developed a similar line of thought in his debate with the "theology of ordinances" ("Die Wahrnehmung der Geschichte in der christlichen Sozialethik," *Evangelische Theologie* 20 [1960], pp. 263-287, esp. pp. 274-280), along the lines of Part I, below. Also W. Dantine in "Die Geschichtlichkeit des Rechtes als ethisches Problem" (*Zeitschrift für Evangelische Ethik* 6 [1962], pp. 321ff.) stressed the significance of history as the decisive criterion for the understanding of law. He developed his thoughts only in reference to the responsibility for the formation of laws.

2. Cf. Chr. Graf von Krockow, *Die Entscheidung* (1958).

3. On this point, cf. the rich contents of the minutes of the Commission on Law by W.-D. Marsch, "Evangelische Theologie vor der Frage nach dem Recht," *Ev. Theol.* 20 (1960), pp. 481ff.

4. E. Brunner, *Das Gebot und die Ordnungen* (1932).

5. P. Althaus, *Theologie der Ordnungen* (1935); H. Thielicke, *Theologische Ethik*, Vol. II (1955); W. Künneth, *Evangelische Ethik des Politischen* (1954).

6. Althaus, *Theologie der Ordnungen*, p. 9.

7. On Bonhoeffer's concept of mandates, see J. Moltmann, *Herrschaft Christi und soziale Wirklichkeit nach Dietrich Bonhoeffer* (1959). The earlier discussion on the subject of the concept of institutions is brought together in Marsch, op. cit., pp. 491-497 (see above, note 3).

8. Moltmann, "Die Wahrnehmung der Geschichte," pp. 271ff.

9. Moltmann has pointed out the significance of history for the basis of Barth's "specific ethic" and the way in which the decisionism of earlier dialectical theology was overcome ("Die Wahrnehmung der Geschichte," pp. 281ff.). It must be admitted that this represents progress beyond the theology of ordinances (p. 283). We should underscore Moltmann's reservation about whether "history can be rightly understood in terms of a vertical intervention and a horizontal context" (ibid.). Moltmann asks whether Barth does not remain close to actualism, and I would ask further whether the idea of the intervention of the Christ event from above does not obscure the horizontal element of history.

10. It should be stated more precisely as "proleptic and doxological structure." Cf. my article "Was ist eine dogmatische Aussage?" *Kerygma und Dogma* 8 (1962), pp. 81-99, esp. pp. 94ff.

11. See my more detailed presentation of my basic position in *Kerygma und Dogma* 5 (1959), p. 231.

12. This must be said in disagreement with the highly instructive lecture by A. Kaufmann, *Naturrecht und Geschichtlichkeit* (1957), pp. 29ff.

13. W. Weischedel, *Recht und Ethik* (2d ed., 1959), p. 33.

14. J. Ellul, *The Theological Foundation of Law* (1948; E.T. 1969).

15. Ernst Wolf, *Königsherrschaft Christi* (1958), pp. 39ff.

16. Cf. R. Aron's critical evaluation of Tönnies in *Deutsche Soziologie der Gegenwart* (1955), p. 23.

17. This phraseology had been used the previous day by W. Maihofer in his address on "Naturrecht und Rechtspositivismus."

18. This is the case in A. Gehlen's work and also in that of A. Portmann.

19. In this connection cf. W. Schulz, *Der Gott der neuzeitlichen Metaphysik* (1959).

20. H. J. Iwand, *Nachgelassene Werke*, Vol. I, *Glauben und Wissen* (1962), pp. 112ff.

21. Used by W. Maihofer in his lecture (see above, note 17).

22. Cf. Klaus Koch, "Spätisraelitisches Geschichtsdenken am Beispiel des Buches Daniel," in *Historische Zeitschrift* 193 (1961), pp. 1-32, esp. p. 24.

23. I Sam. 8:20b: "That our king may govern us and go out before us and fight our battles."

24. G. von Rad, *Theology of the Old Testament*, Vol. I (1957; E.T. 1962), p. 322.

25. This is shown to be the case by O. Plöger in *Theocracy and Eschatology* (E.T. 1968), esp. pp. 19f., 76, 108ff.

26. Bloch's ideas were compared with the basic insights of modern anthropology in W. Maihofer's lecture (see above, note 17), but without a discussion of the theological dimensions considered here.

27. H. Dombois, *Das Recht der Gnade* (1961), pp. 164ff.

28. G. W. F. Hegel, *Phaenomenologie*, ed. Hoffmeister, p. 141.

29. G. W. F. Hegel, *Enzyklopädie*, §490, cf. §484.

30. See G. Rohrmoser, *Subjektivität und Verdinglichung, Theologie und Gesellschaft im Denken des jungen Hegel* (1961), pp. 48ff.; also L. Landgrebe, "Das Problem der Dialektik," in *Marxismusstudien*, 3d series, 1960, pp. 18ff.

31. A retrospective view from this vantage point will discover throughout the history of law the working of creative love, unbeknown to man, in the formation of human societies.

3. THEOLOGY AND THE CRISIS IN ETHICS

This essay was first published in *Theologische Literaturzeitung* 87 (1962), pp. 7-16.

1. Inaugural lecture delivered in Mainz, July 20, 1961.

2. A. Ritschl, *Rechtfertigung und Versöhnung*, Vol. III (3d ed.), §29, pp. 214f. For the influence of Ritschl's students on the changes

in these paragraphs in the third edition, see G. Ecke, *Die theologische Schule Albrecht Ritschls und die evangelische Kirche der Gegenwart*, Vol. I (1897), pp. 42f., 137ff.

3. Herrmann *(Die Religion im Verhältnis zum Welterkennen und zur Sittlichkeit*, 1879) still regarded the Christian faith as the "absolute religion" (pp. 272f.), and his bitterest reproach against Pfleiderer was that the latter had abandoned this position (p. 329, etc.).

4. Ibid., p. 250, etc.

5. W. Herrmann, *Der Verkehr des Christen mit Gott* (1886; 5th ed., 1908), p. 50.

6. R. Bultmann, *Glauben und Verstehen*, Vol. I, p. 106.

7. The title of the famous essay of 1892 had been anticipated in the 1879 book when Herrmann reproached his opponents for failing to "acknowledge in the historical life of Jesus the revelation that God was giving to them" (p. 366; cf. pp. 375, 401). But even then it was for Herrmann no longer a question of "a past historical event," but of the historical "work which Christ was continuing in his church" (p. 379).

8. In 1879 Herrmann did not distinguish between "geschichtlich" and "historisch," as is particularly clear from the position he took toward Fichte's contrast between "historisch" and "metaphysisch" (pp. 399f.), which he simply seems to reverse; but later he agreed with Lessing that it is "impossible to base religious conviction on a historical judgment" *(Der Verkehr des Christen mit Gott*, p. 56). Consequently he made a sharp distinction after this between the historic Christ and historical research. Such research had the task of breaking down "false supports of faith" (p. 60; cf. p. 181). This concession to historical skepticism left his statements about revelation in the historical Christ stranded in an impenetrable fog, and Bultmann merely drew the obvious consequences from this state of affairs.

9. R. Bultmann, *Kirche und Lehre im NT* (1929); *Glauben und Verstehen*, Vol. I, p. 161. Even later Bultmann stressed: "What is said about grace can be understood only by those who know (or can and should know) the demands that the law makes on them" ("Allgemeine Wahrheiten und christliche Verkündigung" [1957], *Glauben und Verstehen*, Vol. III, p. 174).

10. R. Bultmann, "Das christliche Gebot der Nächstenliebe" (1930), *Glauben und Verstehen*, Vol. I, p. 234.

11. K. Barth had weighty reasons for rejecting the subordination of dogmatics to ethics that had been carried out in the name of Rothe and

Ritschl. "Dogmatics itself, indeed all theology, became applied anthropology. The criterion was no longer the word of God, but the idea of the Good, which dominated the search for the excellence of the Christian life and which had been sought and found apart from revelation; the Word of God was drawn on only insofar as it could be made intelligible as the historical medium and vehicle of this idea" (*KD* I/2, pp. 875ff.).

12. F. Gogarten, "Theologie und Geschichte," *Zeitschrift für Theologie und Kirche* (hereafter cited as *ZThK*) 50 (1953), p. 379.

13. E. Fuchs, *Zum hermeneutischen Problem in der Theologie* (1959), pp. 190, 193.

14. Fuchs' isolated emphasis on the mediating function of language at the expense of its declarative function is apparently the result of his intending from the start that his theology of language was to be an interpretation of the Reformation doctrine of law and gospel. Cf. *Zum hermeneutischen Problem*, p. 283.

15. E. Fuchs, *Hermeneutik* (2d ed. 1958), p. 155; cf. p. 147. See also Bultmann's work cited above in note 10.

16. G. Ebeling, "Die Evidenz des Ethischen und die Theologie," *ZThK* 57 (1960), p. 328.

17. In connection with Paul's understanding of law and gospel, Ebeling felt the difficulty, as he himself stressed, that Paul's understanding of law was based on salvation history and was thus different from the Reformers' understanding of law (*ZThK* 55 [1958], p. 286).

18. G. Chr. Storr, *Lehrbuch der christlichen Dogmatik* (1803), regarded religion as essentially based on conscience (§17: "The origin of religion is to be sought in the conscience") and appealed to Kant's moral proof of God (§18), while attempting to combine with it the physicotheological proof. Herrmann himself spoke of the "supernaturalism" of Christianity, but in the sense of the superiority of morality to nature. See Herrmann, *Die Religion im Verhältnis zum Welterkennen und zur Sittlichkeit*, pp. 212f., 218.

19. A. G. Tholuck, *Guido und Julius. Die Lehre von der Sünde und vom Versöhner, oder die wahre Weihe des Zweiflers* (1823), p. 296; cf. p. 301.

20. F. Nietzsche, *Toward a Genealogy of Morals* II, Aphorism 6.

21. Ibid., Aphorisms 16ff.

22. F. Nietzsche, *Human, All-Too-Human*, Aphorism 69.

23. G. Ebeling ("Die Evidenz des Ethischen," p. 323n1), building on a statement by Fritz Heinemann. Cf. G. Ebeling, "Hauptprobleme der protestantischen Theologie in der Gegenwart," *ZThK* 57 (1960), p. 130.

24. Ebeling, "Die Evidenz des Ethischen," p. 334.

25. Ibid., p. 333. A challenge to a "pure feeling of identity with mankind."

26. K. E. Løgstrup, *Die ethische Forderung* (1959), pp. 46f., etc.

27. K. E. Løgstrup, "Ethik und Ontologie," *ZThK* 57 (1960), pp. 368, 373.

28. W. Herrmann has rightly been given credit for discovering this "historicity" of ethical actions; F. Gogarten, "Theologie und Geschichte," *ZThK* 50 (1953), pp. 375, 378f.; R. Bultmann, *Glauben und Verstehen*, Vol. II, p. 234. In Herrmann's thought the contingent, creatively new element of ethical activity in contrast to all prior reality was not yet evident in its general significance for a historical understanding of reality, insofar as it is characterized by the continual appearance of new, contingent events. Nor did it make clear the historicity of ethical action in the total picture of human openness to the world. Cf. my essay in *Studium generale*, 1962, "Wirkungen biblischer Gotteserkenntnis auf das abendländische Menschenbild." For Herrmann these connections remained concealed by his contrast of the ethical realm and the theoretical knowledge of nature. But his discovery of the historicity of human endeavor, even though inadequately formulated, should not be obscured by an approach in terms of situation ethics.

29. Løgstrup's approach in terms of situation ethics cannot be reconciled with his own observations about the "nature of norms, that they stand in a relationship of tension with reality" ("Ethik und Ontologie," p. 374). Moreover, it is quite remarkable that Løgstrup terms the radical demand "speechless" (*Die ethische Forderung*, pp. 21f.) in contrast to the wishes and expectations that are addressed to me and to the social norms (pp. 60f.). Can speechlessness be combined with the concept of a demand? Does not rather the speechlessness of the situation mean that it depends on what the creative human deed makes out of it? and that it does not have the nature of a demand?

30. Fuchs moves from the general statement: "It is language that guarantees or permits being and, in it, that which exists and that which exists as being," to say that "the essence of speech is permission," and

that speech events "grant permission, guarantee freedom, justify being" (*Zum hermeneutischen Problem in der Theologie*, p. 283). It is obvious that here all too quickly the analysis of language is reduced to a modern alternative expression for the traditional concept of justification (cf. also ibid., pp. 191, 193, 220f.). In this way the entire question of the declarative function of language, in which the historical languages have their development, is obscured. The isolation of the mediating function of the word from its declarative function is explicitly carried out by Ebeling ("Wort Gottes und Hermeneutik," *ZThK* 56 [1959], pp. 249f.). But such a distinction is just as problematic as the personalistic distinction between behavior oriented to persons and that oriented to content. Both belong together, just as statement and (personal) communication belong together in language. Only so can there be the concrete reality of historical languages on the one hand and that of personal relationships on the other.

31. Løgstrup, "Ethik und Ontologie," pp. 357ff., esp. p. 373.

32. G. Gloege, "Der theologische Personalismus als dogmatisches Problem," *Kerygma und Dogma* 1 (1955), pp. 23-41, esp. p. 39: "Personal thought presupposes ontological statements."

33. On the basis of the proclamation of law in the history of revelation, cf. R. Rendtorff, *Offenbarung als Geschichte* (1961), pp. 33ff.

34. E. Fuchs (*Hermeneutik*, 2d ed., p. 150) lays claim to Rom. 1:20f. as the basis for his statement that God encounters "all humans through moral demands."

4. An Answer to Gerhard Ebeling

This letter was first published in *Zeitschrift für Theologie und Kirche* 70 (1973), pp. 448-462.

1. Cf. G. Ebeling, "Die Evidenz des Ethischen und die Theologie," *Zeitschrift für Theologie und Kirche* 57 (1960), pp. 318-356, reprinted in *Wort und Glaube* (hereafter cited as *WuG*), Vol. II (1969), pp. 1-41. Also cf. W. Pannenberg, "Die Krise des Ethischen und die Theologie," *Theologische Literaturzeitung* 87 (1962), pp. 7-16 (translated as Chapter 3, above: "Theology and the Crisis in Ethics"). And cf. G. Ebeling, "Die Krise des Ethischen und die Theologie," *WuG* II, pp. 42-55. The letter reprinted here first appeared, together with Ebeling's answer, in *ZThK* 70, 1973 ("Ein Briefwechsel").

2. Ebeling, "Die Krise des Ethischen," *WuG* II, p. 49.

3. Ibid., pp. 48f.

4. Ibid., p. 48.

5. Ibid., p. 49.

6. Ibid., p. 48.

7. The latter seems to be in the foreground when in your essay on the self-evident authority *(Evidenz)* of the ethical you speak of the "ethical problem" (Ebeling, "Die Evidenz des Ethischen," *WuG* II, pp. 9f.) or of the "problem of the ethical" (ibid., p. 10), while the same formulations (ibid., pp. 24f.) refer to the problem that is first created by the ethical itself.

8. Ibid., pp. 14ff.

9. Ibid., pp. 18ff.

10. Here I would like to refer to my sketch in *Theologie und Reich Gottes* (1971), pp. 63ff. (Cf. *Theology and the Kingdom of God* [Westminster Press, 1969], pp. 102ff.)

11. Ebeling, "Die Evidenz des Ethischen," *WuG* II, pp. 9f.

12. Ibid., p. 10.

13. Ebeling, "Die Krise des Ethischen," *WuG* II, p. 47.

14. Ibid.

15. Cf. Pannenberg, "Die Krise des Ethischen," p. 14 (see p. 67 above): "It is only out of each specific understanding of reality as a whole that the basic features of an ethical attitude emerge."

16. Ebeling, "Die Evidenz des Ethischen," *WuG* II, p. 10.

17. I thus agree with you that ethics became autonomous in connection with the "denominational divisions" (ibid., p. 46). Your observation that this involves "a fact which I did not take into account," however, surprises me. What else did it mean when I said (Pannenberg, "Die Krise des Ethischen," p. 12; quoted in *WuG;* see p. 63 above) that it is not only since Nietzsche but earlier that "ethics had already cut itself off from its religious roots in the Christian tradition"?

18. Ebeling, "Die Krise des Ethischen," *WuG* II, p. 44.

19. In your reply you do not dispute this point, which was decisive for the argument of my Mainz lecture, and that would be made even clearer by consideration of Herrmann's position of 1879 in contrast to his later views. You merely stress the distinctive nature of Herrmann's concept of proof, which I had not questioned. Thus I cannot understand what it is on which you base your reprimand that I place

"everything in a false light from the outset" (Ebeling, "Die Krise des Ethischen," *WuG* II, p. 43n.).

20. Ibid., p. 44.

21. Pannenberg, "Die Krise des Ethischen," p. 8 (see p. 58 above).

22. Ebeling, "Die Krise des Ethischen," *WuG* II, p. 45.

23. Ibid., p. 50.

24. Ibid., p. 54.

25. Ibid.

26. Ibid., p. 50.

27. Ebeling, essay in *WuG* I, p. 434.

28. Ibid., pp. 432ff.

29. Ebeling, "Die Krise des Ethischen," *WuG* II, p. 51.

30. Ibid., p. 50.

31. Ibid.

32. Ibid.

33. Ibid.

34. W. Pannenberg, *Grundfragen systematischer Theologie* (1967), pp. 284ff. (E.T. *Basic Questions in Theology,* Vol. II [Fortress Press, 1971], pp. 65-118).

35. Ebeling, "Die Krise des Ethischen," *WuG* II, p. 53.

5. THE BASIS OF ETHICS IN THE THOUGHT OF ERNST TROELTSCH

This essay was first published in W. Pannenberg, *Ethik und Ekklesiologie,* Göttingen, 1977.

1. E. Troeltsch, "Grundprobleme der Ethik, erörtert aus Anlass von Herrmanns Ethik" ("Basic Problems of Ethics Viewed in the Light of Herrmann's Ethics"), *Zeitschrift für Theologie und Kirche,* Vol. 12 (1902), pp. 44-94; 125-178. Reprinted in E. Troeltsch, *Gesammelte Schriften,* Vol. II (1913), pp. 552-672. Page references below are to the original publication in *ZThK.*

2. Troeltsch, "Grundprobleme der Ethik," p. 44. On the following page the "general" ethical problem is similarly described as that "of the ultimate values and goals of human life and activity." This understanding of the theme in teleological and anthropological terms is also found in W. Herrmann's *Ethik* (1901; 5th ed., 1913), §§5f. Herrmann begins with the life situation of the individual by raising the question of the unity of one's own life through "mastery of the feelings by one's consciousness concentrated in *one* idea of the goal," §5, p. 19

(emphasis mine). This approach led him to the concept of the moral good.

3. Troeltsch, "Grundprobleme der Ethik," p. 45. In the preface to the third edition Herrmann expressly confirmed his agreement with Troeltsch on this point. Karl Barth denied this agreement in 1925, but acknowledged it in *Kirchliche Dogmatik* (I/2, p. 879). See W. Groll, *Ernst Troeltsch und Karl Barth—Kontinuität im Widerspruch* (1976), pp. 55f.

4. Troeltsch, "Grundprobleme der Ethik," p. 52.

5. Ibid., p. 55.

6. In his essay "Grundprobleme der Ethik" (1902) Troeltsch saw the presupposition of this transition in both Pietism and Puritanism, and felt it had developed in parallel fashion in England and on the continent (pp. 52ff.). In his *Soziallehren*, however, he acknowledged the specific influence which the "Neo-Calvinism" of the Puritan revolution had on the change in the meaning of ethics, in contrast to Lutheranism. *Die Soziallehren der christlichen Kirchen und Gruppen* (1912), p. 790. For the following summary, see pp. 733ff., 741ff., and esp. pp. 754ff., 762ff.

7. Troeltsch, "Grundprobleme der Ethik," pp. 55f.

8. Ibid., p. 139.

9. Ibid., pp. 134f.

10. Ibid., p. 135.

11. Ibid., p. 139, where this is explicitly stated; cf. pp. 56f.

12. Herrmann, *Ethik*, pp. 12-35 (§§3-9) and pp. 42ff. (§§10-11). The unevenness and gaps in Herrmann's argumentation have been discussed in convincing and subtle manner in Traugott Koch's unpublished *Habilitationsschrift* (Inaugural dissertation at Munich, 1970) entitled "Theologie unter den Bedingungen der Moderne." Koch stresses the inadequate development of the concept of the self in Herrmann (pp. 13ff.), which is not mediated by the concept of goal (pp. 16ff.), so that Herrmann was unable to show that freedom remains a gift (p. 20). Similar questions might be addressed to Troeltsch in reference to his making the ultimate "spirit" independent of the future Lordship of God (see below). Be that as it may, the fruitfulness of Herrmann's approach to the problem of self-assertion is seen particularly in the light of the most recent discussion on the nature of subjectivity. (See the article by D. Henrich in *Subjektivität und Selbsterhaltung, Beiträge zur Diagnose der Moderne*, ed. H. Ebeling,

1976.) Here is the reason for Herrmann's abandoning the question of the highest good, aside from saying that the question cannot be answered (pp. 34f.). Orienting the desire to a good or a goal would imply tracing the desire to a cause and therefore eliminating it as a concept (pp. 36f., §10), that is, removing its autonomy. But can the future be thought of as a sufficient cause?

13. Troeltsch, "Grundprobleme der Ethik," p. 85. T. Koch (Dissertation, pp. 26ff.) agrees with this criticism, which both Troeltsch and Pfleiderer expressed. On the basis of the universality of the "ought" the individual is not united with the other person and the idea of community cannot be achieved.

14. Troeltsch, "Grundprobleme der Ethik," p. 134; cf. pp. 68f.

15. Ibid., pp. 70f.

16. Ibid., pp. 84, 86. Cf. the critical comments on pp. 156f. "Here Herrmann is completely the stern dogmatician and apologete who can believe in the value of Christianity only at the price of the worthlessness of everything non-Christian" (p. 157).

17. Ibid., pp. 78f.

18. Ibid., p. 56.

19. Ibid., p. 80.

20. Ibid., p. 79.

21. Ibid., p. 57.

22. Ibid., p. 58. On Schleiermacher's criticism of Kant on the basis of Plato and the concept of the highest good, see Marlin E. Miller, *Der Übergang. Schleiermachers Theologie des Reiches Gottes im Zusammenhang seines Gesamtdenkens* (1970), pp. 54ff.

23. Troeltsch, "Grundprobleme der Ethik," pp. 58f. Cf. Schleiermacher, *Grundriss der philosophischen Ethik*, ed. A. Twesten (1841), §95.

24. See the discussion of the relationship between Schleiermacher's philosophical and theological ethics in H. J. Birkner, *Schleiermachers christliche Sittenlehre im Zusammenhang seines philosophisch-theologischen Systems* (1964). Birkner brings out the point that "the introduction of Schleiermacher's doctrine of Christian ethics lets any specifics of his own philosophical ethics and its relation to the Christian doctrine of ethics shine through at very few points" (p. 85). He explains this by pointing out that the philosophical ethics was not yet in print, and feels that there is still a "positive relationship between the two disciplines."

25. Troeltsch, "Grundprobleme der Ethik," p. 59.

26. Troeltsch, *Soziallehren*, p. 34.

27. Troeltsch, "Grundprobleme der Ethik," pp. 143f.

28. Ibid., p. 144.

29. Ibid., p. 156.

30. See the discussion of Norman Metzler, *The Ethics of the Kingdom* (Ann Arbor, Mich.: University Microfilms, 1974), pp. 345ff., esp. p. 348. Johannes Weiss, as well as A. Schweitzer, A. von Harnack, and W. Herrmann, was not able to take the insight of the eschatological nature of the future rule of God in the message of Jesus and apply it in his systematic theology, but instead substituted the concept of children of God or a spiritualizing reinterpretation. Troeltsch was able to use J. Weiss's exegetical discovery in a fruitful way in his theology through his ethic of the highest good.

31. W. Herrmann, "Grundprobleme der Ethik," pp. 95ff. On the origins of Herrmann's doctrine of redemption in A. Tholuck and the "theology of renewal," see W. Greive, *Der Grund des Glaubens. Die Christologie Wilhelm Herrmanns* (1976), pp. 91ff.

32. Troeltsch, "Grundprobleme der Ethik," p. 159.

33. Herrmann, *Ethik*, p. 35.

34. Ibid. P. Fischer-Appelt, in his book *Metaphysik im Horizont der Theologie Wilhelm Herrmanns* (1965; pp. 176ff.), explored the original meaning of the religious interpretation of the highest good in Herrmann's early writings, *Die Metaphysik in der Theologie* (Halle, 1876), and *Die Religion im Verhältnis zum Welterkennen und zur Sittlichkeit* (Halle, 1879). These writings form the basis on which it proved impossible to determine precisely the nature of the highest good, with its twofold character as gift and task; but it is in the *Ethik*, where the content of the highest good varies with the situation, that it is impossible to define the concept unambiguously. N. Metzler (*The Ethics of the Kingdom*, p. 309) correctly stresses the difference between Herrmann's approach and the way A. Ritschl combines religion and ethics in the concept of the Kingdom of God as gift and task (see ibid., pp. 178ff.). This probably was also influenced by the interpretation of J. Weiss (ibid., pp. 313ff.). The later Herrmann interpreted Jesus' message of the Kingdom as theocentric but not futuristic, as "the Lordship of God in human beings themselves" (W. Herrmann, *Dogmatik*, ed. M. Rade, 1925; p. 25). For the believer it is also "his highest good," but only as a consequence of obedience to

God's power (ibid.). Does this not reduce the Lordship of God to a metaphor for the authority of the moral law, so that to this extent Herrmann remains in line with Kant's interpretation of the concept, even though he no longer thought of God's Lordship as the result of moral actions?

35. Troeltsch, "Grundprobleme der Ethik," p. 59. Cf. Schleiermacher, *Die Christliche Sitte*, ed. L. Jonas (2d ed., 1884), Vol. I, p. 8 (§§22ff.) and Vol. II, pp. 32ff.; cf. pp. 27f., 75ff.

36. Troeltsch, "Grundprobleme der Ethik," p. 129.

37. The concept of the action of reason on nature is at the center of the "presentation of the concept of moral doctrine" in the final edition of Schleiermacher's philosophical ethics (*Grundriss der philosophischen Ethik*, ed. Twesten, "Allgemeine Einleitung" [1816], §§62ff. = *Ausgewählte Werke*, ed. O. Braun and J. Bauer, Vol. II [1927; 2d ed., 1967], pp. 537ff.). The distinction among the concepts of the good, virtue, and duty was worked out in the following section on the "Formulation of the Doctrine of Morality" (*Grundriss*, ed. Twesten, §§110ff.; *Werke*, Vol. II, pp. 550ff.). In the following the paragraph numbers refer to the introduction to the 1816 edition. On the concept of the highest good, see M. E. Miller, *Der Übergang*, pp. 54ff.

38. In his lecture on ethics, 1812/13, Schleiermacher said that in the idea of the highest good, "producing and what is produced are regarded as identical." On the other hand the highest good is the "result" of all actions performed in accordance with duty (*Werke*, Vol. II, p. 256 [§87] and p. 406 [§2]). Here Schleiermacher seems deliberately to avoid the concept of goal, as indicated in an 1827 note to the passage. (Cf. the comments of M. E. Miller, *Der Übergang*, p. 138, on the avoidance of the concept of goal in reference to the Kingdom of God.) Schleiermacher made explicit statements as early as 1803 in "Grundlinien einer Kritik der bisherigen Sittenlehre," criticizing the description of the good as a goal, as if "the deed were only the means, and the work or the result the final goal" (*Werke*, Vol. I, p. 169). And in his academy lectures of 1827 on the concept of the highest good, Schleiermacher attacked the "highly unnatural separation of the ways of action and activity from the results that they produce" (*Werke*, Vol. I, p. 450). His comment is directed against the one-sided modern treatment of ethics in terms of duty and virtue, and by contrast he could demonstrate the superiority of the ancient ethic of

the highest good in that examples of the good "always represent something that has resulted from human activity but at the same time include the results and advance them" (ibid., p. 456). Thus the concept of the good eliminates the one-sidedness of a doctrine of mere duty or virtue. And it can be said of the highest good that it is everything, and that it includes everything" (ibid., p. 470).

39. In contrast to the concepts of virtue and duty, it is only in the concept of the highest good that the unity of reason with nature is "established as producing and produced." (*Grundriss der philosophischen Ethik*, "Allgemeine Einleitung" [1816], in *Werke*, Vol. II, p. 509 [§114]. Cf. the lectures of 1812/13 in *Grundriss*, ed. Twesten, p. 257 [§86] = *Werke*, Vol. II, p. 256 [§87].)

40. Schleiermacher, *Grundriss*, ed. Twesten, pp. 44f. ("Lehre vom höchsten Gut" §19 = *Werke*, Vol. II, p. 569). In his second academy lecture of 1827 Schleiermacher formulated four varying expressions of the highest good as the completion of moral activity, corresponding to the four types of activity: (1) eternal peace and (2) the golden age represent the completion of organizational activity according to its general and its particular aspect; (3) the completed community of knowledge and (4) the "Kingdom of Heaven" represent the completion of symbolic activity. It is, however, only in the mutual interaction of all of them together that the highest good is accomplished (*Werke*, Vol. II, pp. 480ff. = *Sämtliche Werke*, Vol. III/2, pp. 481ff.; see Miller, *Der Übergang*, pp. 75ff.).

41. Schleiermacher, *Die christliche Sitte*, ed. L. Jonas (Berlin, 1884), Vol. II, p. 78. On the correspondence of the theological concept of the Kingdom of God and the concept of the Kingdom of Heaven developed in Schleiermacher's philosophical ethics, see Miller, *Der Übergang*, pp. 228ff.

42. Ibid., pp. 291f.; cf. Miller, *Der Übergang*, pp. 198ff. In Schleiermacher's *Glaubenslehre* the Kingdom of God is described as founded by Christ (§117 topic sentence), based on redemption (§46 supplement) and constituting the new life of the believer in its totality (cf. §113, 4; §114, 2). In this sense I can accept Miller's thesis that the theology of the *Glaubenslehre* is conceived of "as a theology of the Kingdom of God." Miller rightly stresses that for Schleiermacher the Kingdom of God is not merely the goal or purpose of ethical acts, but that it is active in the total life of the church in reference to its origin, existence, and completion (pp. 137ff.).

43. Schleiermacher, *Die christliche Sitte*, Vol. II, p. 13.

44. Troeltsch, *Die Absolutheit des Christentums und die Religionsgeschichte* (2d ed., 1912), p. 127; cf. p. 131.

45. Ibid., pp. 98f. See also Troeltsch, *Soziallehren*, p. 979. "The idea of the future Kingdom of God is no other than the idea of the final realization of the absolute, however that may be pictured. It does not, as shortsighted critics claim, rob the world and worldly life of value, but it punishes the powers and through all transitions makes the soul strong in its assurance of a final, future, absolute meaning and goal of human effort. The conclusion of this idea constitutes the famous sentence, later taken up by Barth, "The other world is the power of this world."

46. Ibid., p. 100.

47. Ibid., p. 98.

48. Troeltsch, "Grundprobleme der Ethik," p. 150.

49. E. Troeltsch, "Die christliche Weltanschauung und die wissenschaftlichen Gegenströmungen" ("The Christian World View and the Scientific Countercurrents"), *ZThK* 3 (1893), pp. 493-528; 4 (1894), pp. 167-231 (= *Gesammelte Schriften*, Vol. II, pp. 227-327).

50. Troeltsch, "Die christliche Weltanschauung," *ZThK* 3 (1893), pp. 518f.

51. Troeltsch, "Die Selbstständigkeit der Religion," *ZThK* 5 (1895), pp. 388f.; cf. pp. 390f. The ideal "perceptions of spiritual realities" are grasped, in contrast to sense perceptions, only "in the inseparable accompaniment of energetic feelings that lay hold on the whole person, in relative independence of the participation and commitment of the will, which must take form and shape for them."

52. Ibid., p. 396. Cf. the entire passage, pp. 392-397, as well as *ZThK* 6 (1896), p. 179, where similarly the "power that confronts" the consciousness "with specific ideal demands" is characterized as the distinctive nature of the "religious object."

53. Compare the way in which, according to Schleiermacher, we "pull back" the consciousness of absolute dependence to the concept of God as the "source" of the dependence. That is, the concept of God goes back to the "most direct reflection" on the feeling of dependence and does not condition this feeling or produce it (*Der christliche Glaube* [2d ed., 1830], §4, 4).

54. Troeltsch, "Die Selbstständigkeit der Religion," p. 392.

55. E. Troeltsch, "Geschichte and Metaphysik," *ZThK* 8 (1898), p. 30; cf. pp. 28ff., 55.

56. Ibid., p. 28. Cf. p. 42, where Troeltsch states further that there is "a final and concluding goal that is set for" the development that proceeds from this interaction.

57. Troeltsch, *Absolutheit,* p. 56; cf. "Geschichte und Metaphysik," pp. 30ff.

58. In *Wissenschaftstheorie und Theologie* (1973; E.T. *Theology and the Philosophy of Science,* Westminster Press, 1976), pp. 106ff., I put the relationship to Dilthey in the foreground and in comparison to Dilthey's hermeneutical interpretation of history, I criticized the prominence of the concept of goal in Troeltsch as a "narrowing to a perspective characterized by a theory of action" (p. 107; cf. pp. 111f.). But from another point of view, especially in relation to Schleiermacher, the concept of purpose represents the transcendence of the content toward which human actions strive, in contrast to the completion of the action itself. In terms of a hermeneutic of an experience of meaning prior to the action, this concept could be developed in a more highly differentiated and more relevant manner than is possible in terms of the concept of goal.

59. Troeltsch, *Absolutheit,* pp. 56f. Note the catchword *"gleichartig"* ("similarly"), p. 60. Cf. also "Geschichte und Metaphysik," p. 38, *Gesammelte Schriften,* Vol. II, pp. 745f., and *Psychologie und Erkenntnistheorie in der Religionswissenschaft* (1905), p. 9.

60. Troeltsch, *Absolutheit,* p. 57.

61. Ibid., p. 65. On the "converging tendencies" in the development, cf. pp. 68f.

62. Ibid., pp. 57f.; cf. pp. 68ff., 100, 148.

63. Ibid., p. 48, cf. p. 64.

64. Ibid., p. 68.

65. Troeltsch, "Geschichte und Metaphysik," p. 41.

66. Ibid., pp. 44f.

67. Troeltsch, *Absolutheit,* p. 70; cf. pp. 68f.

68. Ibid., pp. 69, 80, 146; cf. pp. 99f. and Troeltsch, "Die christliche Weltanschauung," p. 526.

69. Troeltsch, *Der Historismus und seine Überwindung,* ed. F. von Hügel (1924), p. 82.

70. Troeltsch, "Grundprobleme der Ethik," p. 151.

71. Ibid., p. 153.

72. Ibid., p. 154.

73. It needs to be supplemented only in reference to the message of

Jesus, through which the presence of God's future salvation was experienced in him. This feature gained in importance as the expectation of the nearness of its fulfillment faded and it developed into the doctrine of the incarnation. Troeltsch always was aware of this in reference to the role of the concept of redemption (ibid., p. 160).

74. Ibid., p. 154; cf. pp. 163ff.

75. Ibid., pp. 167f.

76. Ibid., p. 169.

77. Ibid., pp. 171ff.; cf. p 164.

78. The expression "compromise" is seldom found (e.g., Troeltsch, *Soziallehren*, pp. 90, 116), but it occurs in the highly important passage in the retrospective summary of the period of the early church, pp. 179f.

79. Troeltsch, *Soziallehren*, pp. 422ff.; cf. pp. 179f.

80. See the summary of the entire work, pp. 972ff.

81. As is well known, H. Richard Niebuhr, in a quiet departure from the position of his teacher Troeltsch, formulated the Christian task in contrast to secular culture in the last of the different types of relationships he outlined in *Christ and Culture* (Harper & Brothers, 1951). A readiness to compromise is rightly demanded wherever the finite interests of individuals and groups come into conflict with each other. The infinite interests of God and his Lordship, however, admit no compromise that would violate the First Commandment. Differing human views of God and his Lordship might in their relativity be subject to the duty to compromise, but God's Lordship itself is not.

82. The concluding section of the *Soziallehren*, with its emphasis on the idea that the Kingdom of God is "within us" (p. 986), constitutes a remarkable contrast to the line of thought that is dominant elsewhere in Troeltsch's statements about the Kingdom. Characteristically, however, as used by Troeltsch, this "within us" is ambiguous, not only as the "inwardness" of God's future within us, but at the same time—or primarily?—as the "inwardness" of the intellectual productivity of "all humanity," even though motivated by Christian principles.

83. This point of view has already been touched on in my *Wissenschaftstheorie und Theologie* (1973; *Theology and the Philosophy of Science*), pp. 111f.

84. Troeltsch, "Grundprobleme der Ethik," p. 168; cf. p. 170.

85. Ibid., pp. 164f., 170.

86. Ibid., p. 170; cf. Troeltsch, *Soziallehren*, pp. 30ff.

87. Ibid., p. 151.
88. Ibid., p. 158; cf. pp. 131f.
89. Cf. the discussion by W. Groll, *Ernst Troeltsch und Karl Barth*, pp. 106ff., of Barth's interpretation of Troeltsch's statement, "The other world is the power of this world"; esp. pp. 116ff.

6. LUTHER'S DOCTRINE OF THE TWO KINGDOMS

This essay was first published in W. Pannenberg, *Gottesreich und Menschenreich*, Regensburg, 1972.

1. K. Barth, *Eine Schweizer Stimme* (Zurich, 1945), p. 122. The references that follow in the text are to this work.
2. Thus Luther in his sermon, "Dass man Kinder zur Schulen halten soll" (1530), WA 30 II, 537, 22ff.
3. "Von weltlicher Obrigkeit" (1523), WA 11, 278f. The following page references are to this work.
4. On the concept of "fairness" *(Billigkeit)* in Luther cf. WA 19, 631f. ("Ob Kriegsleute auch in seligem Stande sein können," 1526), and U. Duchrow, *Christenheit und Weltverantwortung. Traditionsgeschichte und systematische Struktur der Zweireichelehre* (1970), pp. 498f. On the question of natural law in Luther, see E. Wolf, "Zur Frage des Naturrechts bei Thomas von Aquin und Luther," in *Peregrinatio*, 1954, pp. 183-213.
5. WA 51, 242.
6. E. Troeltsch, *Gesammelte Schriften*, Vol. I, pp. 485ff.
7. Duchrow, op. cit., pp. 542f., seems to express a similar uneasiness when he writes that the reference to the motivation for Christians to assume secular office is not adequate, since under such circumstances the Sermon on the Mount would remain irrelevant to the political activity of Christians. It is questionable whether his reference, following G. Scharffenorth, to a relationship of Luther's general statements on the then current juristic discussion of the abolition of a Reich Institute of Feuds would be helpful here, even if this context were more solid. The question of the relationship between an individual's motivation and his function in a role determined by the structure of society is not affected by this at all. Nor was the problem first posed by "modern bourgeois reality" and its dualism of private and public life (p. 548), but it has a more fundamental sociological character.
8. WA 11, 249.

9. G. Scharffenorth, *Römer 13 in der Geschichte des politischen Denkens* (Heidelberg dissertation, 1964). U. Duchrow (op. cit., pp. 523ff.) agrees with this work.

10. See H. von Campenhausen, "Augustin und der Fall von Rom," in *Tradition und Leben. Kräfte der Kirchengeschichte. Aufsätze und Vorträge* (1960), pp. 253ff.

11. This is connected with the Platonic distinction (also adopted by Paul) between the inner person (reason), and the outer person characterized by sensual motives. See Duchrow, op. cit., pp. 61ff.

12. Ibid., pp. 486ff., 506ff., 511ff.

13. "Duo sunt quippe, imperator auguste, quibus principaliter mundus hic regitur, auctoritas sacrata pontificium et regalis potestas, in quibus tanto gravius pondus est sacerdotum quanto etiam pro ipsis regibus hominum in divino reddituri sunt examine rationem" (Mirbt-Aland, *Quellen zur Geschichte des Papsttums*, Vol. I [6th ed., 1967], p. 222, no. 462). The influence of this statement on the medieval discussions was mediated through its adoption into the text of the Pseudo-Isidorian Decretals and the Decretum Gratiani. See bibliography in Duchrow, op. cit., p. 328.

14. It was only in the high Middle Ages during the investiture controversy that the popes were successful in claiming for themselves the title "Vicar of Christ."

15. Duchrow, op. cit., p. 335. Alcuin also termed the emperor "teacher" (*doctor*) and "preacher" (*praedicator*) of Christendom (ibid., fn. 52).

16. Ibid., p. 378. Note the principle of the Canon Law of the twelfth century: "Rex, imperator in regno suo, superiorem in temporalibus non recognoscit."

17. Alanus ab Insulis: "Et quod dictum est de imperatore, dictum habeatur de quolibet rege vel principe, qui nulli subest, unusquisque enim tantum iuris habet in regno suo, quantum imperator in imperio" (Duchrow, op. cit., p. 397).

18. Duchrow (op. cit., pp. 258ff.) is probably too quick to regard this thesis as insignificant.

7. The Nation and Humanity

Delivered at the twelfth national convention of the Protestant Working Group of the CDU/CSU (Christian Democratic Union Party and Christian Socialist Union Party), in Bonn, May 27, 1965. First published in *Monatschrift für Pastoraltheologie* 54 (1965), pp. 333-347.

1. Origen, *Contra Celsus* II, 3.

2. Eusebius, *Demonstratio evangelica* VII, 2, 22.

3. John Robinson, from whose congregation in Holland the first Pilgrim Fathers went to America in 1620, held that in spite of all the bad experiences of previous history a democratic congregational life was possible among Christians, because they all shared in the kingship and priesthood of Christ. Cf. G. P. Gooch, *English Democratic Ideas in the 17th Century* (1898; 2d ed., 1927; repr. Harper & Brothers, Harper Torchbooks, 1959), pp. 65f.; cf. pp. 230f. on George Fox.

4. G. Leibholz holds that "the actually existing differences among persons appear today as 'nonessential,' as 'insignificant,' in comparison to the attributes which bind them to each other" (*Strukturprobleme der modernen Democratie* [Karlsruhe, 1958], p. 86). Leibholz is mistaken, however, when he traces *this* concept of equality to Christian ideas.

5. Cf. W.-D. Marsch, *Christlicher Glaube und demokratisches Ethos, dargestellt am Lebenswerk Abraham Lincolns* (Hamburg, 1958), pp. 200f., fn. 42.

6. This means that political education must be accorded a prominent place in the organization of social life. This agrees with the Christian idea that all are equally *called* to achieve true humanity.

7. Cf. H. von Campenhausen, "Augustin und der Fall von Rom," in *Weltgeschichte und Gottesgericht* (Stuttgart, 1947), pp. 2ff.

8. Cf. H. Lowe, *Von Theoderich dem Grossen zu Karl dem Grossen* (Darmstadt, 1958), pp. 18ff.

9. See R. Wittram, *Das Nationale als europäisches Problem* (Göttingen, 1954), esp. pp. 109-148, "Kirche und Nationalismus."

10. This concept has recently found expression in theological discussion in A. Evertz, *Der Abfall der evangelischen Kirche vom Vaterland* (Velbert/Kettwig, 1964), esp. pp. 23ff.

11. Thus P. Althaus, *Grundriss der Ethik* (Gütersloh, 2d ed., 1953), p. 125. Similarly Evertz, *Abfall*, pp. 12ff., etc. Althaus recognizes that there is a limit to this imperative in special circumstances in the lives of individuals and peoples. But how are its applicability and limits determined?

12. The idea of a forced resettlement of the population now living in

the eastern regions has been repeatedly rejected by the representatives of the former German territories in the East, most recently in their congress in Bonn, March 22, 1964. It is hard to understand how efforts for a restitution of old property rights can be reconciled with this position. Above all, it cannot be expected that any Polish government could agree on the basis of a voluntary recognition of old German rights to a revision of the present boundary much less to a restoration of the 1937 boundaries. Possible German efforts to gain from Poland restitution for damages or resettlement rights for refugees could have any chance of success at all only if the present boundaries are recognized.

8. The Peace of God and World Peace

This lecture was first published in *Frieden. Vorlesungen auf dem 13. Deutschen Evangelischen Kirchentag Hannover 1967*, Berlin, 1967.

9. The Future and the Unity of Mankind

This lecture was first published in *Evangelische Theologie* 32 (1972), pp. 384-402.

1. At the conference on "Hope and the Future of Man" in New York in October 1971, for which this lecture was prepared, there was particular interest in conversation between the eschatologically oriented German participants and American theologians and philosophers whose starting point was the thought of Teilhard de Chardin or Whitehead's process philosophy.

2. On this issue in Teilhard's thought, see my remarks in *Acta Teilhardiana VIII* (1971), pp. 5ff. ("Spirit and Energy"), esp. pp. 8f.

3. Cf. J. B. Cobb, *God and the World* (Westminster Press, 1969).

4. J. B. Cobb, *A Christian Natural Theology* (Westminster Press, 1965), pp. 203ff.

5. Thus for example, C. F. von Weizsäcker, *Bedingungen des Friedens* (1964), pp. 15f., and his similar but more cautious statement, "Zumutungen des Friedens," in *Streit um den Frieden*, ed. W. Beck and R. Schmid (1967), pp. 31ff., esp. pp. 41ff.

6. A. Toffler, *Future Shock* (Bantam Books, 1971), p. 15.

7. E. Fromm, *The Revolution of Hope: Toward a Humanized*

Technology (Harper & Row, 1968), p. 29; cf. p. 41. Fromm borrowed the idea from Lewis Mumford.

8. According to Whitehead, all permanent reality consists of chains of momentary "occasions" or "events," which constitute the ultimate elements of all reality, the individual "actual entities" (A. N. Whitehead, *Process and Reality* [Macmillan Co., 1929], passim).

9. These are the "eternal objects" of Whitehead's philosophy.

10. E. Fromm, *The Revolution of Hope*, pp. 62ff.

11. E. Voegelin, *Die neue Wissenschaft der Politik* (2d ed., 1965, pp. 83ff.), accepts this state of affairs in the concept of representation.